Affirmations For Money

Affirmations For Money

Troy Sterling

Published by Troy Sterling, 2024.

While every precaution has been taken in the preparation of this book, the publisher assumes no responsibility for errors or omissions, or for damages resulting from the use of the information contained herein.

AFFIRMATIONS FOR MONEY

First edition. March 6, 2024.

Copyright © 2024 Troy Sterling.

ISBN: 979-8224418480

Written by Troy Sterling.

I am a magnet for financial well-being and security.
I am grateful for the financial prosperity that fills my life.
Money comes to me in abundance, and I use it wisely.
I am open to receiving financial miracles with gratitude.
I am deserving of all the prosperity life has to offer.
I am a magnet for financial opportunities, and I welcome them.
I attract financial success with every positive thought.
I am in tune with the energy of abundance and prosperity.
I am a magnet for wealth and abundance in every area of my life.
Financial prosperity is my natural state of being.
I am open to receiving wealth in expected and unexpected ways.
Money flows to me easily, and I welcome it with open arms.
I am a magnet for financial success and positive outcomes.
I am aligned with the vibration of financial abundance.
I attract wealth effortlessly and joyfully.
I am open to the limitless possibilities of financial success.
I am deserving of all the prosperity life has to offer.
I am a magnet for financial opportunities, and I welcome them.
I attract financial success with every positive thought.
I am in tune with the energy of abundance and prosperity.
I am a magnet for wealth and abundance in every area of my life.
Financial prosperity is my natural state of being.
I am open to receiving wealth in expected and unexpected ways.
Money flows to me easily, and I welcome it with open arms.
I am a magnet for financial success and positive outcomes.
I am aligned with the vibration of financial abundance.
I attract wealth effortlessly and joyfully.
I am open to the limitless possibilities of financial success.
Wealth and success are drawn to me, and I welcome them joyfully.
I am worthy of a life filled with financial abundance.
Money is a tool that empowers me to live my best life.
I am open to receiving wealth from diverse and creative sources.
Financial success is a natural expression of my positive energy.
I attract financial opportunities effortlessly and naturally.
Money flows to me easily, and I use it wisely.

I am aligned with the energy of abundance and financial well-being.
I attract positive and abundant financial experiences.
I am a magnet for attracting financial success and fulfillment.
I am grateful for the wealth and abundance in my life.
Money comes to me in abundance, and I use it wisely.
I am open to receiving financial miracles with gratitude.
I am open to receiving wealth from known and unknown sources.
I am a magnet for financial security and stability.
Financial success is mine to claim, and I claim it now.
I attract wealth by staying focused on my goals and aspirations.
My mind is attuned to the frequency of financial prosperity.
I am a channel through which wealth flows effortlessly.
I attract financial success with every positive thought I think.
I am worthy of receiving unlimited wealth and abundance.
Money is a positive and abundant part of my life.
I welcome financial success into every area of my life.
I am open to receiving unlimited prosperity and abundance.
I am a magnet for financial prosperity, and it flows to me effortlessly.
My financial success inspires others to pursue their dreams.
I am open to receiving unexpected windfalls of money with joy.
I am a magnet for financial opportunities that align with my purpose.
Money flows to me easily, and I am open to receiving it.
I am grateful for the financial blessings that enrich my life.
I am a conduit for financial abundance, and it flows through me.

I attract wealth with grace and gratitude, creating a positive cycle.
I am aligned with the universal flow of prosperity and success.
Financial opportunities are drawn to me like a magnet.
My financial situation is improving beyond my wildest dreams.
I trust in my ability to create unlimited wealth and abundance.
I attract financial success with ease and joy.
Wealth flows into my life like a river, carrying blessings.
I am open to receiving wealth in ways beyond my imagination.

I am a magnet for lucrative opportunities that align with my goals.

My wealth grows as I invest in my personal and professional development.

I release any fear of financial limitations and embrace abundance.

I am financially free, allowing me to live life on my terms.

Money is a positive force in my life, providing limitless possibilities.

I am in harmony with the energy of wealth and abundance.

I attract prosperity with every positive thought I cultivate.

Wealth is an integral part of my life, and it manifests effortlessly.

I am open to receiving wealth from unlimited sources.

My thoughts about money create a reality of prosperity.

I am a magnet for financial success, and I welcome it graciously.

Money is a tool for positive transformation in my life and the world.

I attract financial opportunities effortlessly and gracefully.

Wealth is my natural state, and I allow it to flow abundantly.

I am a money magnet, attracting wealth from all directions.

My financial success is a reflection of my positive mindset.

Abundance is drawn to me, and I accept it with gratitude.

Money is a resource that allows me to live life to the fullest.

I am deserving of all the wealth and prosperity life offers.

My bank account is a reservoir of abundance, constantly replenishing.

My financial goals are ambitious, and I achieve them with ease.

I attract money with love and gratitude, and it multiplies.

I am aligned with the energy of prosperity and success.

Money is a positive force, and I use it to create positive change.

My income grows consistently, allowing me to fulfill my dreams.

I am a magnet for financial opportunities that elevate my life.

Wealth is my constant companion, guiding me to new heights.

I attract financial security and abundance with each breath.

I release any resistance to receiving wealth and embrace abundance.

My financial wealth allows me to contribute to the well-being of others.

I am a wise steward of my resources, making empowered choices.

I am a magnet for financial wisdom and make sound investment decisions.

I attract lucrative opportunities that align with my purpose.

Money is a source of joy and fulfillment in my life.

My bank account is a reflection of the positive energy I radiate.

I trust in the process of wealth creation and enjoy every step.

Abundance is my birthright, and I claim it with confidence.

I am open to receiving unexpected financial blessings with grace.

Every day, in every way, I am growing richer and richer.

My positive mindset attracts abundance in all its forms.

Financial success enhances every aspect of my well-being.

I am grateful for the wealth that flows into my life effortlessly.

Financial prosperity is my natural state of being.

I am open to receiving wealth in expected and unexpected ways.

Money flows to me easily, and I welcome it with open arms.

I am a magnet for financial success and positive outcomes.

I am aligned with the vibration of financial abundance.

I attract wealth effortlessly and joyfully.

I am open to the limitless possibilities of financial success.

I am a magnet for financial well-being and security.

I am grateful for the financial prosperity that fills my life.
Money comes to me in abundance, and I use it wisely.
I am open to receiving financial miracles with gratitude.
My financial abundance allows me to live a life of generosity.
Wealth flows effortlessly into my life, bringing prosperity.
I am a magnet for financial success and positive outcomes.
I am aligned with the vibration of financial abundance.
I attract wealth effortlessly and joyfully.
I am open to the limitless possibilities of financial success.
I am a magnet for financial well-being and security.
I am grateful for the financial prosperity that fills my life.
Money comes to me in abundance, and I use it wisely.
I am open to receiving financial miracles with gratitude.
I am deserving of all the prosperity life has to offer.
I am a magnet for financial opportunities, and I welcome them.
I attract financial success with every positive thought.
I am in tune with the energy of abundance and prosperity.
I am a magnet for wealth and abundance in every area of my life.
I am open to the limitless possibilities of financial success.
I am a magnet for financial well-being and security.
I am grateful for the financial prosperity that fills my life.
Money comes to me in abundance, and I use it wisely.
I am open to receiving financial miracles with gratitude.
I am deserving of all the prosperity life has to offer.
I am a magnet for financial opportunities, and I welcome them.
I attract financial success with every positive thought.
I am in tune with the energy of abundance and prosperity.
I am a magnet for wealth and abundance in every area of my life.
Financial prosperity is my natural state of being.
I am open to receiving wealth in expected and unexpected ways.
Money flows to me easily, and I welcome it with open arms.
I am open to receiving financial miracles with gratitude.
I am deserving of all the prosperity life has to offer.
I am a magnet for financial opportunities, and I welcome them.
I attract financial success with every positive thought.

I am in tune with the energy of abundance and prosperity.
I am a magnet for wealth and abundance in every area of my life.
Financial prosperity is my natural state of being.
I am open to receiving wealth in expected and unexpected ways.
Money flows to me easily, and I welcome it with open arms.
I am a magnet for financial success and positive outcomes.
I am aligned with the vibration of financial abundance.
I attract wealth effortlessly and joyfully.
I attract financial success with every positive thought.
I am in tune with the energy of abundance and prosperity.
I am a magnet for wealth and abundance in every area of my life.
Financial prosperity is my natural state of being.
I am open to receiving wealth in expected and unexpected ways.
Money flows to me easily, and I welcome it with open arms.
I am a magnet for financial success and positive outcomes.
I am aligned with the vibration of financial abundance.
I attract wealth effortlessly and joyfully.
I am open to the limitless possibilities of financial success.
I am a magnet for financial well-being and security.
I am grateful for the financial prosperity that fills my life.
Money comes to me in abundance, and I use it wisely.
I am grateful for the abundance that fills every area of my life.
I attract wealth and success with every positive thought.
Money flows to me effortlessly, and I welcome it with gratitude.
I am a magnet for financial success and positive outcomes.
I am aligned with the vibration of financial abundance.
I attract wealth effortlessly and joyfully.
I am open to the limitless possibilities of financial success.
I am a magnet for financial well-being and security.
I am grateful for the financial prosperity that fills my life.
Money comes to me in abundance, and I use it wisely.
I am open to receiving financial miracles with gratitude.
I am deserving of all the prosperity life has to offer.
I am a magnet for financial opportunities, and I welcome them.
I am open to receiving unexpected windfalls of money with gratitude.

I am deserving of all the wealth and success that comes my way.
I am financially free, and my life is filled with abundance.
I attract prosperity by maintaining a positive mindset.
Wealth is drawn to me, and I welcome it with open arms.
My positive thoughts about money create positive financial outcomes.
I am a magnet for financial miracles, and I welcome them into my life.
I am a money magnet, attracting abundance with ease.
Financial success is my birthright, and I claim it now.
My bank account is a reflection of my positive and prosperous thoughts.
I release any limiting beliefs about money and embrace my financial power.
I am open to receiving wealth beyond my wildest dreams.
Money is a tool that amplifies my positive impact on the world.
I attract financial opportunities effortlessly and naturally.
Every dollar I spend circulates and comes back to me multiplied.
My financial goals are achievable, and I pursue them with determination.
I release all fear and doubt about money, embracing abundance.
I am a wise steward of my finances, making sound and beneficial decisions.
My income is constantly increasing, and I welcome financial growth.
I am a magnet for lucrative opportunities that lead to wealth.
Financial success is a journey, and I am on the path to prosperity.
I attract wealth by consistently providing value to others.
Money comes to me effortlessly, supporting my dreams and desires.
I attract financial opportunities that align with my passions.
My wealth expands as I contribute positively to the world.
Money is a powerful force for good in my life and the lives of others.
I am open to receiving wealth from known and unknown channels.
I radiate confidence in my ability to accumulate wealth.
Financial prosperity is a natural outcome of my positive mindset.
I am a magnet for abundance, attracting it effortlessly.
I trust that the universe is conspiring to bring me financial success.
My thoughts are in alignment with the frequency of wealth.
Wealth flows to me in expected and unexpected ways.
I am a beacon of prosperity, attracting limitless abundance.
I am a magnet for financial success and positive outcomes.
I am aligned with the vibration of financial abundance.

I attract wealth effortlessly and joyfully.
I am open to the limitless possibilities of financial success.
I am a magnet for financial well-being and security.
I am grateful for the financial prosperity that fills my life.
Money comes to me in abundance, and I use it wisely.
I am open to receiving financial miracles with gratitude.
I am deserving of all the prosperity life has to offer.
I am a magnet for financial opportunities, and I welcome them.
I attract financial success with every positive thought.
I am in tune with the energy of abundance and prosperity.
I am a magnet for wealth and abundance in every area of my life.
I am deserving of all the prosperity life has to offer.

I am a magnet for financial opportunities, and I welcome them.
I attract financial success with every positive thought.
I am in tune with the energy of abundance and prosperity.
I am a magnet for wealth and abundance in every area of my life.
Financial prosperity is my natural state of being.
I am open to receiving wealth in expected and unexpected ways.
Money flows to me easily, and I welcome it with open arms.
I am a magnet for financial success and positive outcomes.
I am aligned with the vibration of financial abundance.
I attract wealth effortlessly and joyfully.
I am open to the limitless possibilities of financial success.
I am a magnet for financial well-being and security.
I am grateful for the financial prosperity that fills my life.
Money comes to me in abundance, and I use it wisely.
I am open to receiving financial miracles with gratitude.
I am deserving of all the prosperity life has to offer.
I am a magnet for financial opportunities, and I welcome them.
I attract financial success with every positive thought.
I am in tune with the energy of abundance and prosperity.
I am a magnet for wealth and abundance in every area of my life.
Financial prosperity is my natural state of being.
I am open to receiving wealth in expected and unexpected ways.
Money flows to me easily, and I welcome it with open arms.
I am in tune with the energy of abundance and prosperity.
I am a magnet for wealth and abundance in every area of my life.
Financial prosperity is my natural state of being.
I am open to receiving wealth in expected and unexpected ways.
Money flows to me easily, and I welcome it with open arms.
I am a magnet for financial success and positive outcomes.
I am aligned with the vibration of financial abundance.
I attract wealth effortlessly and joyfully.
I am open to the limitless possibilities of financial success.
I am a magnet for financial well-being and security.
I am grateful for the financial prosperity that fills my life.
Money comes to me in abundance, and I use it wisely.

I am open to receiving financial miracles with gratitude.

I attract financial opportunities that align with my purpose.

I am open to receiving wealth from diverse and creative sources.

Money flows to me easily, and I use it wisely.

I am aligned with the energy of abundance and financial well-being.

I attract positive and abundant financial experiences.

I am a magnet for attracting financial success and fulfillment.

I am grateful for the wealth and abundance in my life.

Money comes to me in abundance, and I use it to create positive change.

I am open to receiving financial miracles with gratitude.

I am deserving of all the prosperity life has to offer.

I am a magnet for financial opportunities, and I welcome them.

I attract financial success with every positive thought.

I attract wealth by staying focused on my goals and aspirations.

My mind is attuned to the frequency of financial prosperity.

I am a channel through which wealth flows effortlessly.

I attract financial success with every breath I take.

I am worthy of receiving unlimited wealth and abundance.

Money is a positive and abundant part of my life.

I welcome financial success into every area of my life.

I am open to receiving unlimited prosperity and abundance.

I am a magnet for financial prosperity, and it flows to me effortlessly.

Wealth and success are drawn to me, and I welcome them joyfully.

I am deserving of all the financial prosperity that comes my way.

My thoughts about money create a positive and abundant reality.

I welcome financial blessings with open arms and gratitude.

My financial situation is improving beyond my wildest dreams.

I trust the process of wealth creation and abundance.

I attract money with love and positive intentions.

Financial opportunities are drawn to me like a magnet.

I release any fear or doubt about my ability to accumulate wealth.

My wealth is a reflection of my positive thoughts and actions.

I attract prosperity by maintaining a mindset of abundance.

Money is a tool that empowers me to live my best life.

I am open to receiving wealth from known and unknown sources.

I am a magnet for attracting financial security and stability.
Financial success is mine to claim, and I claim it now.
My financial success serves as inspiration for others.
I trust in my ability to create unlimited wealth.
Money is a positive force, and it enriches every aspect of my life.
I am in harmony with the energy of financial well-being.
I am a magnet for attracting lucrative financial opportunities.
I am open to receiving unexpected windfalls of money.
My bank account reflects the abundance in my life.
I am grateful for the wealth that continuously manifests for me.
I am aligned with the universal flow of prosperity.
Money comes to me easily, and I am open to receiving it.
I attract financial success with every positive thought I think.
I am a magnet for wealth, and I allow it to flow freely.
Wealth constantly flows into my life with ease.
I trust that the universe is conspiring to bring me wealth.
I am open to receiving money from various channels.
My financial mindset is one of prosperity and abundance.
I attract financial opportunities effortlessly and naturally.
I am a magnet for positive financial outcomes.
Money is a source of joy and fulfillment in my life.
I welcome financial prosperity as a constant companion.
My wealth is a reflection of the value I provide to the world.
I attract wealth with grace and gratitude.
Financial success is my destiny, and I embrace it fully.
I am open to receiving wealth in ways I may not have imagined.
Abundance flows to me, and I am deserving of it.
I attract financial opportunities that align with my passions.
Money comes to me in abundance, and I use it wisely.
I am open to receiving financial miracles with gratitude.
I am deserving of all the prosperity life has to offer.
I am a magnet for financial opportunities, and I welcome them.
I attract financial success with every positive thought.
I am in tune with the energy of abundance and prosperity.
I am a magnet for wealth and abundance in every area of my life.

Financial prosperity is my natural state of being.
I am open to receiving wealth in expected and unexpected ways.
Money flows to me easily, and I welcome it
Opportunities for financial growth are abundant in my life.
I radiate confidence in my ability to attract wealth.
My financial goals are achievable and within reach.
Wealth and success are drawn to me, and I welcome them joyfully.
I am worthy of a life filled with financial abundance.
Money is a tool that empowers me to live my best life.
I am open to receiving wealth from diverse and creative sources.
Financial success is a natural expression of my positive energy.
I attract financial opportunities effortlessly and naturally.
Money flows to me easily, and I use it wisely.
I am aligned with the energy of abundance and financial well-being.
I attract positive and abundant financial experiences.
I am a magnet for attracting financial success and fulfillment.
I am grateful for the wealth and abundance in my life.
Money comes to me in abundance, and I use it wisely.
I am open to receiving financial miracles with gratitude.
I am open to receiving wealth from known and unknown sources.
I am a magnet for financial security and stability.
Financial success is mine to claim, and I claim it now.
I attract wealth by staying focused on my goals and aspirations.
My mind is attuned to the frequency of financial prosperity.
I am a channel through which wealth flows effortlessly.
I attract financial success with every positive thought I think.
I am worthy of receiving unlimited wealth and abundance.
Money is a positive and abundant part of my life.
I welcome financial success into every area of my life.
I am open to receiving unlimited prosperity and abundance.
I am a magnet for financial prosperity, and it flows to me effortlessly.
My financial success inspires others to pursue their dreams.
I am open to receiving unexpected windfalls of money with joy.
I am a magnet for financial opportunities that align with my purpose.
Money flows to me easily, and I am open to receiving it.

I am grateful for the financial blessings that enrich my life.

I am a conduit for financial abundance, and it flows through me.

I attract wealth with grace and gratitude, creating a positive cycle.

I am aligned with the universal flow of prosperity and success.

Financial opportunities are drawn to me like a magnet.

My financial situation is improving beyond my wildest dreams.

I trust in my ability to create unlimited wealth and abundance.

I attract financial success with ease and joy.

Wealth flows into my life like a river, carrying blessings.

I am open to receiving wealth in ways beyond my imagination.

I am a magnet for lucrative opportunities that align with my goals.

My wealth grows as I invest in my personal and professional development.

I release any fear of financial limitations and embrace abundance.

I am financially free, allowing me to live life on my terms.

Money is a positive force in my life, providing limitless possibilities.

I am in harmony with the energy of wealth and abundance.

I attract prosperity with every positive thought I cultivate.

Wealth is an integral part of my life, and it manifests effortlessly.

I am open to receiving wealth from unlimited sources.

My thoughts about money create a reality of prosperity.

I am a magnet for financial success, and I welcome it graciously.

Money is a tool for positive transformation in my life and the world.

I attract financial opportunities effortlessly and gracefully.

Wealth is my natural state, and I allow it to flow abundantly.

I am a money magnet, attracting wealth from all directions.

My financial success is a reflection of my positive mindset.

Abundance is drawn to me, and I accept it with gratitude.

Money is a resource that allows me to live life to the fullest.

I am deserving of all the wealth and prosperity life offers.

My bank account is a reservoir of abundance, constantly replenishing.

My financial goals are ambitious, and I achieve them with ease.

I attract money with love and gratitude, and it multiplies.

I am aligned with the energy of prosperity and success.

Money is a positive force, and I use it to create positive change.

My income grows consistently, allowing me to fulfill my dreams.

I am a magnet for financial opportunities that elevate my life.

Wealth is my constant companion, guiding me to new heights.

I attract financial security and abundance with each breath.

I release any resistance to receiving wealth and embrace abundance.

My financial wealth allows me to contribute to the well-being of others.

I am a wise steward of my resources, making empowered choices.

I am a magnet for financial wisdom and make sound investment decisions.

I attract lucrative opportunities that align with my purpose.

Money is a source of joy and fulfillment in my life.

My bank account is a reflection of the positive energy I radiate.

I trust in the process of wealth creation and enjoy every step.

Abundance is my birthright, and I claim it with confidence.

I am open to receiving unexpected financial blessings with grace.

Every day, in every way, I am growing richer and richer.

My positive mindset attracts abundance in all its forms.

Financial success enhances every aspect of my well-being.

I am grateful for the wealth that flows into my life effortlessly.

Financial prosperity is my natural state of being.

I am open to receiving wealth in expected and unexpected ways.

Money flows to me easily, and I welcome it with open arms.

I am a magnet for financial success and positive outcomes.

I am aligned with the vibration of financial abundance.

I attract wealth effortlessly and joyfully.

I am open to the limitless possibilities of financial success.

I am a magnet for financial well-being and security.

I am grateful for the financial prosperity that fills my life.

Money comes to me in abundance, and I use it wisely.

I am open to receiving financial miracles with gratitude.

My financial abundance allows me to live a life of generosity.

Wealth flows effortlessly into my life, bringing prosperity.

I am a magnet for financial success and positive outcomes.

I am aligned with the vibration of financial abundance.

I attract wealth effortlessly and joyfully.

I am open to the limitless possibilities of financial success.

I am a magnet for financial well-being and security.

I am grateful for the financial prosperity that fills my life.
Money comes to me in abundance, and I use it wisely.
I am open to receiving financial miracles with gratitude.
I am deserving of all the prosperity life has to offer.
I am a magnet for financial opportunities, and I welcome them.
I attract financial success with every positive thought.
I am in tune with the energy of abundance and prosperity.
I am a magnet for wealth and abundance in every area of my life.
I am open to the limitless possibilities of financial success.
I am a magnet for financial well-being and security.
I am grateful for the financial prosperity that fills my life.
Money comes to me in abundance, and I use it wisely.
I am open to receiving financial miracles with gratitude.

I am deserving of all the prosperity life has to offer.
I am a magnet for financial opportunities, and I welcome them.
I attract financial success with every positive thought.
I am in tune with the energy of abundance and prosperity.
I am a magnet for wealth and abundance in every area of my life.
Financial prosperity is my natural state of being.
I am open to receiving wealth in expected and unexpected ways.
Money flows to me easily, and I welcome it with open arms.
I am open to receiving financial miracles with gratitude.
I am deserving of all the prosperity life has to offer.
I am a magnet for financial opportunities, and I welcome them.
I attract financial success with every positive thought.
I am in tune with the energy of abundance and prosperity.
I am a magnet for wealth and abundance in every area of my life.
Financial prosperity is my natural state of being.
I am open to receiving wealth in expected and unexpected ways.
Money flows to me easily, and I welcome it with open arms.
I am a magnet for financial success and positive outcomes.
I am aligned with the vibration of financial abundance.
I attract wealth effortlessly and joyfully.
I attract financial success with every positive thought.
I am in tune with the energy of abundance and prosperity.
I am a magnet for wealth and abundance in every area of my life.
Financial prosperity is my natural state of being.
I am open to receiving wealth in expected and unexpected ways.
Money flows to me easily, and I welcome it with open arms.
I am a magnet for financial success and positive outcomes.
I am aligned with the vibration of financial abundance.
I attract wealth effortlessly and joyfully.
I am open to the limitless possibilities of financial success.
I am a magnet for financial well-being and security.
I am grateful for the financial prosperity that fills my life.
Money comes to me in abundance, and I use it wisely.
I am grateful for the abundance that fills every area of my life.
I attract wealth and success with every positive thought.

Money flows to me effortlessly, and I welcome it with gratitude.
I am a magnet for financial success and positive outcomes.
I am aligned with the vibration of financial abundance.
I attract wealth effortlessly and joyfully.
I am open to the limitless possibilities of financial success.
I am a magnet for financial well-being and security.
I am grateful for the financial prosperity that fills my life.
Money comes to me in abundance, and I use it wisely.
I am open to receiving financial miracles with gratitude.
I am deserving of all the prosperity life has to offer.
I am a magnet for financial opportunities, and I welcome them.
I am open to receiving unexpected windfalls of money with gratitude.
I am deserving of all the wealth and success that comes my way.
I am financially free, and my life is filled with abundance.
I attract prosperity by maintaining a positive mindset.
Wealth is drawn to me, and I welcome it with open arms.
My positive thoughts about money create positive financial outcomes.
I am a magnet for financial miracles, and I welcome them into my life.
I am a money magnet, attracting abundance with ease.
Financial success is my birthright, and I claim it now.
My bank account is a reflection of my positive and prosperous thoughts.
I release any limiting beliefs about money and embrace my financial power.
I am open to receiving wealth beyond my wildest dreams.
Money is a tool that amplifies my positive impact on the world.
I attract financial opportunities effortlessly and naturally.
Every dollar I spend circulates and comes back to me multiplied.
My financial goals are achievable, and I pursue them with determination.
I release all fear and doubt about money, embracing abundance.
I am a wise steward of my finances, making sound and beneficial decisions.
My income is constantly increasing, and I welcome financial growth.
I am a magnet for lucrative opportunities that lead to wealth.
Financial success is a journey, and I am on the path to prosperity.
I attract wealth by consistently providing value to others.

Money comes to me effortlessly, supporting my dreams and desires.

I attract financial opportunities that align with my passions.
My wealth expands as I contribute positively to the world.
Money is a powerful force for good in my life and the lives of others.
I am open to receiving wealth from known and unknown channels.
I radiate confidence in my ability to accumulate wealth.
Financial prosperity is a natural outcome of my positive mindset.
I am a magnet for abundance, attracting it effortlessly.
I trust that the universe is conspiring to bring me financial success.
My thoughts are in alignment with the frequency of wealth.
Wealth flows to me in expected and unexpected ways.
I am a beacon of prosperity, attracting limitless abundance.
I am a magnet for financial success and positive outcomes.
I am aligned with the vibration of financial abundance.
I attract wealth effortlessly and joyfully.
I am open to the limitless possibilities of financial success.
I am a magnet for financial well-being and security.
I am grateful for the financial prosperity that fills my life.
Money comes to me in abundance, and I use it wisely.
I am open to receiving financial miracles with gratitude.
I am deserving of all the prosperity life has to offer.
I am a magnet for financial opportunities, and I welcome them.
I attract financial success with every positive thought.
I am in tune with the energy of abundance and prosperity.
I am a magnet for wealth and abundance in every area of my life.
I am deserving of all the prosperity life has to offer.
I am a magnet for financial opportunities, and I welcome them.
I attract financial success with every positive thought.
I am in tune with the energy of abundance and prosperity.
I am a magnet for wealth and abundance in every area of my life.
Financial prosperity is my natural state of being.
I am open to receiving wealth in expected and unexpected ways.
Money flows to me easily, and I welcome it with open arms.
I am a magnet for financial success and positive outcomes.
I am aligned with the vibration of financial abundance.
I attract wealth effortlessly and joyfully.

I am open to the limitless possibilities of financial success.
I am a magnet for financial well-being and security.
I am grateful for the financial prosperity that fills my life.
Money comes to me in abundance, and I use it wisely.
I am open to receiving financial miracles with gratitude.
I am deserving of all the prosperity life has to offer.
I am a magnet for financial opportunities, and I welcome them.
I attract financial success with every positive thought.
I am in tune with the energy of abundance and prosperity.
I am a magnet for wealth and abundance in every area of my life.
Financial prosperity is my natural state of being.
I am open to receiving wealth in expected and unexpected ways.
Money flows to me easily, and I welcome it with open arms.
I am in tune with the energy of abundance and prosperity.
I am a magnet for wealth and abundance in every area of my life.
Financial prosperity is my natural state of being.
I am open to receiving wealth in expected and unexpected ways.
Money flows to me easily, and I welcome it with open arms.
I am a magnet for financial success and positive outcomes.
I am aligned with the vibration of financial abundance.
I attract wealth effortlessly and joyfully.
I am open to the limitless possibilities of financial success.
I am a magnet for financial well-being and security.
I am grateful for the financial prosperity that fills my life.
Money comes to me in abundance, and I use it wisely.
I am open to receiving financial miracles with gratitude.
I attract financial opportunities that align with my purpose.
I am open to receiving wealth from diverse and creative sources.
Money flows to me easily, and I use it wisely.
I am aligned with the energy of abundance and financial well-being.
I attract positive and abundant financial experiences.
I am a magnet for attracting financial success and fulfillment.
I am grateful for the wealth and abundance in my life.
Money comes to me in abundance, and I use it to create positive change.
I am open to receiving financial miracles with gratitude.

I am deserving of all the prosperity life has to offer.
I am a magnet for financial opportunities, and I welcome them.
I attract financial success with every positive thought.
I attract wealth by staying focused on my goals and aspirations.
My mind is attuned to the frequency of financial prosperity.
I am a channel through which wealth flows effortlessly.
I attract financial success with every breath I take.
I am worthy of receiving unlimited wealth and abundance.
Money is a positive and abundant part of my life.
I welcome financial success into every area of my life.
I am open to receiving unlimited prosperity and abundance.
I am a magnet for financial prosperity, and it flows to me effortlessly.
Wealth and success are drawn to me, and I welcome them joyfully.
I am deserving of all the financial prosperity that comes my way.
My thoughts about money create a positive and abundant reality.
I welcome financial blessings with open arms and gratitude.
My financial situation is improving beyond my wildest dreams.
I trust the process of wealth creation and abundance.
I attract money with love and positive intentions.
Financial opportunities are drawn to me like a magnet.
I release any fear or doubt about my ability to accumulate wealth.
My wealth is a reflection of my positive thoughts and actions.
I attract prosperity by maintaining a mindset of abundance.
Money is a tool that empowers me to live my best life.
I am open to receiving wealth from known and unknown sources.
I am a magnet for attracting financial security and stability.
Financial success is mine to claim, and I claim it now.
My financial success serves as inspiration for others.
I trust in my ability to create unlimited wealth.
Money is a positive force, and it enriches every aspect of my life.
I am in harmony with the energy of financial well-being.
I am a magnet for attracting lucrative financial opportunities.
I am open to receiving unexpected windfalls of money.
My bank account reflects the abundance in my life.
I am grateful for the wealth that continuously manifests for me.

I am aligned with the universal flow of prosperity.
Money comes to me easily, and I am open to receiving it.
I attract financial success with every positive thought I think.
I am a magnet for wealth, and I allow it to flow freely.
Wealth constantly flows into my life with ease.
I trust that the universe is conspiring to bring me wealth.
I am open to receiving money from various channels.
My financial mindset is one of prosperity and abundance.
I attract financial opportunities effortlessly and naturally.
I am a magnet for positive financial outcomes.
Money is a source of joy and fulfillment in my life.
I welcome financial prosperity as a constant companion.
My wealth is a reflection of the value I provide to the world.
I attract wealth with grace and gratitude.
Financial success is my destiny, and I embrace it fully.
I am open to receiving wealth in ways I may not have imagined.
Abundance flows to me, and I am deserving of it.
I attract financial opportunities that align with my passions.
Money comes to me in abundance, and I use it wisely.
I am open to receiving financial miracles with gratitude.
I am deserving of all the prosperity life has to offer.
I am a magnet for financial opportunities, and I welcome them.
I attract financial success with every positive thought.
I am in tune with the energy of abundance and prosperity.
I am a magnet for wealth and abundance in every area of my life.
Financial prosperity is my natural state of being.
I am open to receiving wealth in expected and unexpected ways.
Money flows to me easily, and I welcome it
Opportunities for financial growth are abundant in my life.
I radiate confidence in my ability to attract wealth.
My financial goals are achievable and within reach.
Wealth and success are drawn to me, and I welcome them joyfully.
I am worthy of a life filled with financial abundance.
Money is a tool that empowers me to live my best life.
I am open to receiving wealth from diverse and creative sources.

Financial success is a natural expression of my positive energy.

I attract financial opportunities effortlessly and naturally.

Money flows to me easily, and I use it wisely.

I am aligned with the energy of abundance and financial well-being.

I attract positive and abundant financial experiences.

I am a magnet for attracting financial success and fulfillment.

I am grateful for the wealth and abundance in my life.

Money comes to me in abundance, and I use it wisely.

I am open to receiving financial miracles with gratitude.

I am open to receiving wealth from known and unknown sources.

I am a magnet for financial security and stability.

Financial success is mine to claim, and I claim it now.

I attract wealth by staying focused on my goals and aspirations.

My mind is attuned to the frequency of financial prosperity.

I am a channel through which wealth flows effortlessly.

I attract financial success with every positive thought I think.

I am worthy of receiving unlimited wealth and abundance.

Money is a positive and abundant part of my life.

I welcome financial success into every area of my life.

I am open to receiving unlimited prosperity and abundance.

I am a magnet for financial prosperity, and it flows to me effortlessly.

My financial success inspires others to pursue their dreams.

I am open to receiving unexpected windfalls of money with joy.

I am a magnet for financial opportunities that align with my purpose.

Money flows to me easily, and I am open to receiving it.

I am grateful for the financial blessings that enrich my life.

I am a conduit for financial abundance, and it flows through me.

I attract wealth with grace and gratitude, creating a positive cycle.

I am aligned with the universal flow of prosperity and success.

Financial opportunities are drawn to me like a magnet.

My financial situation is improving beyond my wildest dreams.

I trust in my ability to create unlimited wealth and abundance.

I attract financial success with ease and joy.
Wealth flows into my life like a river, carrying blessings.
I am open to receiving wealth in ways beyond my imagination.
I am a magnet for lucrative opportunities that align with my goals.
My wealth grows as I invest in my personal and professional development.
I release any fear of financial limitations and embrace abundance.
I am financially free, allowing me to live life on my terms.
Money is a positive force in my life, providing limitless possibilities.
I am in harmony with the energy of wealth and abundance.
I attract prosperity with every positive thought I cultivate.
Wealth is an integral part of my life, and it manifests effortlessly.
I am open to receiving wealth from unlimited sources.
My thoughts about money create a reality of prosperity.
I am a magnet for financial success, and I welcome it graciously.
Money is a tool for positive transformation in my life and the world.
I attract financial opportunities effortlessly and gracefully.
Wealth is my natural state, and I allow it to flow abundantly.
I am a money magnet, attracting wealth from all directions.
My financial success is a reflection of my positive mindset.
Abundance is drawn to me, and I accept it with gratitude.
Money is a resource that allows me to live life to the fullest.
I am deserving of all the wealth and prosperity life offers.
My bank account is a reservoir of abundance, constantly replenishing.
My financial goals are ambitious, and I achieve them with ease.
I attract money with love and gratitude, and it multiplies.
I am aligned with the energy of prosperity and success.
Money is a positive force, and I use it to create positive change.
My income grows consistently, allowing me to fulfill my dreams.
I am a magnet for financial opportunities that elevate my life.
Wealth is my constant companion, guiding me to new heights.
I attract financial security and abundance with each breath.
I release any resistance to receiving wealth and embrace abundance.
My financial wealth allows me to contribute to the well-being of others.
I am a wise steward of my resources, making empowered choices.
I am a magnet for financial wisdom and make sound investment decisions.

I attract lucrative opportunities that align with my purpose.
Money is a source of joy and fulfillment in my life.
My bank account is a reflection of the positive energy I radiate.
I trust in the process of wealth creation and enjoy every step.
Abundance is my birthright, and I claim it with confidence.
I am open to receiving unexpected financial blessings with grace.
Every day, in every way, I am growing richer and richer.
My positive mindset attracts abundance in all its forms.
Financial success enhances every aspect of my well-being.
I am grateful for the wealth that flows into my life effortlessly.
Financial prosperity is my natural state of being.
I am open to receiving wealth in expected and unexpected ways.
Money flows to me easily, and I welcome it with open arms.
I am a magnet for financial success and positive outcomes.
I am aligned with the vibration of financial abundance.
I attract wealth effortlessly and joyfully.
I am open to the limitless possibilities of financial success.
I am a magnet for financial well-being and security.
I am grateful for the financial prosperity that fills my life.
Money comes to me in abundance, and I use it wisely.
I am open to receiving financial miracles with gratitude.
My financial abundance allows me to live a life of generosity.
Wealth flows effortlessly into my life, bringing prosperity.
I am a magnet for financial success and positive outcomes.
I am aligned with the vibration of financial abundance.
I attract wealth effortlessly and joyfully.
I am open to the limitless possibilities of financial success.
I am a magnet for financial well-being and security.
I am grateful for the financial prosperity that fills my life.
Money comes to me in abundance, and I use it wisely.
I am open to receiving financial miracles with gratitude.
I am deserving of all the prosperity life has to offer.
I am a magnet for financial opportunities, and I welcome them.
I attract financial success with every positive thought.
I am in tune with the energy of abundance and prosperity.

I am a magnet for wealth and abundance in every area of my life.
I am open to the limitless possibilities of financial success.
I am a magnet for financial well-being and security.
I am grateful for the financial prosperity that fills my life.
Money comes to me in abundance, and I use it wisely.
I am open to receiving financial miracles with gratitude.
I am deserving of all the prosperity life has to offer.
I am a magnet for financial opportunities, and I welcome them.
I attract financial success with every positive thought.
I am in tune with the energy of abundance and prosperity.
I am a magnet for wealth and abundance in every area of my life.
Financial prosperity is my natural state of being.
I am open to receiving wealth in expected and unexpected ways.
Money flows to me easily, and I welcome it with open arms.
I am open to receiving financial miracles with gratitude.
I am deserving of all the prosperity life has to offer.
I am a magnet for financial opportunities, and I welcome them.
I attract financial success with every positive thought.
I am in tune with the energy of abundance and prosperity.
I am a magnet for wealth and abundance in every area of my life.
Financial prosperity is my natural state of being.
I am open to receiving wealth in expected and unexpected ways.
Money flows to me easily, and I welcome it with open arms.
I am a magnet for financial success and positive outcomes.
I am aligned with the vibration of financial abundance.
I attract wealth effortlessly and joyfully.
I attract financial success with every positive thought.
I am in tune with the energy of abundance and prosperity.
I am a magnet for wealth and abundance in every area of my life.
Financial prosperity is my natural state of being.
I am open to receiving wealth in expected and unexpected ways.
Money flows to me easily, and I welcome it with open arms.
I am a magnet for financial success and positive outcomes.
I am aligned with the vibration of financial abundance.
I attract wealth effortlessly and joyfully.

I am open to the limitless possibilities of financial success.
I am a magnet for financial well-being and security.
I am grateful for the financial prosperity that fills my life.
Money comes to me in abundance, and I use it wisely.
I am grateful for the abundance that fills every area of my life.
I attract wealth and success with every positive thought.
Money flows to me effortlessly, and I welcome it with gratitude.
I am a magnet for financial success and positive outcomes.
I am aligned with the vibration of financial abundance.
I attract wealth effortlessly and joyfully.
I am open to the limitless possibilities of financial success.
I am a magnet for financial well-being and security.
I am grateful for the financial prosperity that fills my life.
Money comes to me in abundance, and I use it wisely.
I am open to receiving financial miracles with gratitude.
I am deserving of all the prosperity life has to offer.
I am a magnet for financial opportunities, and I welcome them.
I am open to receiving unexpected windfalls of money with gratitude.
I am deserving of all the wealth and success that comes my way.
I am financially free, and my life is filled with abundance.
I attract prosperity by maintaining a positive mindset.
Wealth is drawn to me, and I welcome it with open arms.
My positive thoughts about money create positive financial outcomes.
I am a magnet for financial miracles, and I welcome them into my life.
I am a money magnet, attracting abundance with ease.
Financial success is my birthright, and I claim it now.
My bank account is a reflection of my positive and prosperous thoughts.
I release any limiting beliefs about money and embrace my financial power.
I am open to receiving wealth beyond my wildest dreams.
Money is a tool that amplifies my positive impact on the world.
I attract financial opportunities effortlessly and naturally.
Every dollar I spend circulates and comes back to me multiplied.
My financial goals are achievable, and I pursue them with determination.
I release all fear and doubt about money, embracing abundance.
I am a wise steward of my finances, making sound and beneficial decisions.

My income is constantly increasing, and I welcome financial growth.
I am a magnet for lucrative opportunities that lead to wealth.
Financial success is a journey, and I am on the path to prosperity.
I attract wealth by consistently providing value to others.
Money comes to me effortlessly, supporting my dreams and desires.
I attract financial opportunities that align with my passions.
My wealth expands as I contribute positively to the world.
Money is a powerful force for good in my life and the lives of others.
I am open to receiving wealth from known and unknown channels.
I radiate confidence in my ability to accumulate wealth.
Financial prosperity is a natural outcome of my positive mindset.
I am a magnet for abundance, attracting it effortlessly.
I trust that the universe is conspiring to bring me financial success.
My thoughts are in alignment with the frequency of wealth.
Wealth flows to me in expected and unexpected ways.
I am a beacon of prosperity, attracting limitless abundance.
I am a magnet for financial success and positive outcomes.
I am aligned with the vibration of financial abundance.
I attract wealth effortlessly and joyfully.
I am open to the limitless possibilities of financial success.
I am a magnet for financial well-being and security.
I am grateful for the financial prosperity that fills my life.
Money comes to me in abundance, and I use it wisely.
I am open to receiving financial miracles with gratitude.
I am deserving of all the prosperity life has to offer.
I am a magnet for financial opportunities, and I welcome them.
I attract financial success with every positive thought.
I am in tune with the energy of abundance and prosperity.
I am a magnet for wealth and abundance in every area of my life.
I am deserving of all the prosperity life has to offer.
I am a magnet for financial opportunities, and I welcome them.
I attract financial success with every positive thought.
I am in tune with the energy of abundance and prosperity.
I am a magnet for wealth and abundance in every area of my life.
Financial prosperity is my natural state of being.

I am open to receiving wealth in expected and unexpected ways.
Money flows to me easily, and I welcome it with open arms.
I am a magnet for financial success and positive outcomes.
I am aligned with the vibration of financial abundance.
I attract wealth effortlessly and joyfully.
I am open to the limitless possibilities of financial success.
I am a magnet for financial well-being and security.
I am grateful for the financial prosperity that fills my life.
Money comes to me in abundance, and I use it wisely.
I am open to receiving financial miracles with gratitude.
I am deserving of all the prosperity life has to offer.
I am a magnet for financial opportunities, and I welcome them.
I attract financial success with every positive thought.
I am in tune with the energy of abundance and prosperity.
I am a magnet for wealth and abundance in every area of my life.
Financial prosperity is my natural state of being.
I am open to receiving wealth in expected and unexpected ways.
Money flows to me easily, and I welcome it with open arms.
I am in tune with the energy of abundance and prosperity.
I am a magnet for wealth and abundance in every area of my life.
Financial prosperity is my natural state of being.
I am open to receiving wealth in expected and unexpected ways.
Money flows to me easily, and I welcome it with open arms.
I am a magnet for financial success and positive outcomes.
I am aligned with the vibration of financial abundance.
I attract wealth effortlessly and joyfully.
I am open to the limitless possibilities of financial success.
I am a magnet for financial well-being and security.
I am grateful for the financial prosperity that fills my life.
Money comes to me in abundance, and I use it wisely.
I am open to receiving financial miracles with gratitude.
I attract financial opportunities that align with my purpose.
I am open to receiving wealth from diverse and creative sources.
Money flows to me easily, and I use it wisely.
I am aligned with the energy of abundance and financial well-being.

I attract positive and abundant financial experiences.
I am a magnet for attracting financial success and fulfillment.
I am grateful for the wealth and abundance in my life.
Money comes to me in abundance, and I use it to create positive change.
I am open to receiving financial miracles with gratitude.
I am deserving of all the prosperity life has to offer.
I am a magnet for financial opportunities, and I welcome them.
I attract financial success with every positive thought.
I attract wealth by staying focused on my goals and aspirations.
My mind is attuned to the frequency of financial prosperity.
I am a channel through which wealth flows effortlessly.
I attract financial success with every breath I take.
I am worthy of receiving unlimited wealth and abundance.
Money is a positive and abundant part of my life.
I welcome financial success into every area of my life.
I am open to receiving unlimited prosperity and abundance.
I am a magnet for financial prosperity, and it flows to me effortlessly.
Wealth and success are drawn to me, and I welcome them joyfully.
I am deserving of all the financial prosperity that comes my way.
My thoughts about money create a positive and abundant reality.
I welcome financial blessings with open arms and gratitude.
My financial situation is improving beyond my wildest dreams.
I trust the process of wealth creation and abundance.
I attract money with love and positive intentions.
Financial opportunities are drawn to me like a magnet.
I release any fear or doubt about my ability to accumulate wealth.
My wealth is a reflection of my positive thoughts and actions.
I attract prosperity by maintaining a mindset of abundance.
Money is a tool that empowers me to live my best life.
I am open to receiving wealth from known and unknown sources.
I am a magnet for attracting financial security and stability.
Financial success is mine to claim, and I claim it now.
My financial success serves as inspiration for others.
I trust in my ability to create unlimited wealth.
Money is a positive force, and it enriches every aspect of my life.

I am in harmony with the energy of financial well-being.
I am a magnet for attracting lucrative financial opportunities.
I am open to receiving unexpected windfalls of money.
My bank account reflects the abundance in my life.
I am grateful for the wealth that continuously manifests for me.
I am aligned with the universal flow of prosperity.
Money comes to me easily, and I am open to receiving it.
I attract financial success with every positive thought I think.
I am a magnet for wealth, and I allow it to flow freely.
Wealth constantly flows into my life with ease.
I trust that the universe is conspiring to bring me wealth.
I am open to receiving money from various channels.
My financial mindset is one of prosperity and abundance.
I attract financial opportunities effortlessly and naturally.
I am a magnet for positive financial outcomes.
Money is a source of joy and fulfillment in my life.
I welcome financial prosperity as a constant companion.
My wealth is a reflection of the value I provide to the world.
I attract wealth with grace and gratitude.
Financial success is my destiny, and I embrace it fully.
I am open to receiving wealth in ways I may not have imagined.
Abundance flows to me, and I am deserving of it.
I attract financial opportunities that align with my passions.
Money comes to me in abundance, and I use it wisely.
I am open to receiving financial miracles with gratitude.
I am deserving of all the prosperity life has to offer.
I am a magnet for financial opportunities, and I welcome them.
I attract financial success with every positive thought.
I am in tune with the energy of abundance and prosperity.
I am a magnet for wealth and abundance in every area of my life.
Financial prosperity is my natural state of being.
I am open to receiving wealth in expected and unexpected ways.
Money flows to me easily, and I welcome it
Opportunities for financial growth are abundant in my life.
I radiate confidence in my ability to attract wealth.

My financial goals are achievable and within reach.
Wealth and success are drawn to me, and I welcome them joyfully.
I am worthy of a life filled with financial abundance.
Money is a tool that empowers me to live my best life.
I am open to receiving wealth from diverse and creative sources.
Financial success is a natural expression of my positive energy.
I attract financial opportunities effortlessly and naturally.
Money flows to me easily, and I use it wisely.
I am aligned with the energy of abundance and financial well-being.
I attract positive and abundant financial experiences.
I am a magnet for attracting financial success and fulfillment.
I am grateful for the wealth and abundance in my life.
Money comes to me in abundance, and I use it wisely.
I am open to receiving financial miracles with gratitude.
I am open to receiving wealth from known and unknown sources.
I am a magnet for financial security and stability.
Financial success is mine to claim, and I claim it now.
I attract wealth by staying focused on my goals and aspirations.
My mind is attuned to the frequency of financial prosperity.
I am a channel through which wealth flows effortlessly.
I attract financial success with every positive thought I think.
I am worthy of receiving unlimited wealth and abundance.
Money is a positive and abundant part of my life.
I welcome financial success into every area of my life.
I am open to receiving unlimited prosperity and abundance.
I am a magnet for financial prosperity, and it flows to me effortlessly.
My financial success inspires others to pursue their dreams.
I am open to receiving unexpected windfalls of money with joy.
I am a magnet for financial opportunities that align with my purpose.
Money flows to me easily, and I am open to receiving it.
I am grateful for the financial blessings that enrich my life.
I am a conduit for financial abundance, and it flows through me.
I attract wealth with grace and gratitude, creating a positive cycle.
I am aligned with the universal flow of prosperity and success.
Financial opportunities are drawn to me like a magnet.

My financial situation is improving beyond my wildest dreams.
I trust in my ability to create unlimited wealth and abundance.
I attract financial success with ease and joy.
Wealth flows into my life like a river, carrying blessings.
I am open to receiving wealth in ways beyond my imagination.
I am a magnet for lucrative opportunities that align with my goals.
My wealth grows as I invest in my personal and professional development.
I release any fear of financial limitations and embrace abundance.
I am financially free, allowing me to live life on my terms.
Money is a positive force in my life, providing limitless possibilities.
I am in harmony with the energy of wealth and abundance.
I attract prosperity with every positive thought I cultivate.
Wealth is an integral part of my life, and it manifests effortlessly.
I am open to receiving wealth from unlimited sources.
My thoughts about money create a reality of prosperity.
I am a magnet for financial success, and I welcome it graciously.
Money is a tool for positive transformation in my life and the world.
I attract financial opportunities effortlessly and gracefully.
Wealth is my natural state, and I allow it to flow abundantly.
I am a money magnet, attracting wealth from all directions.
My financial success is a reflection of my positive mindset.
Abundance is drawn to me, and I accept it with gratitude.
Money is a resource that allows me to live life to the fullest.
I am deserving of all the wealth and prosperity life offers.
My bank account is a reservoir of abundance, constantly replenishing.
My financial goals are ambitious, and I achieve them with ease.
I attract money with love and gratitude, and it multiplies.
I am aligned with the energy of prosperity and success.
Money is a positive force, and I use it to create positive change.
My income grows consistently, allowing me to fulfill my dreams.
I am a magnet for financial opportunities that elevate my life.
Wealth is my constant companion, guiding me to new heights.
I attract financial security and abundance with each breath.
I release any resistance to receiving wealth and embrace abundance.
My financial wealth allows me to contribute to the well-being of others.

I am a wise steward of my resources, making empowered choices.
I am a magnet for financial wisdom and make sound investment decisions.
I attract lucrative opportunities that align with my purpose.
Money is a source of joy and fulfillment in my life.
My bank account is a reflection of the positive energy I radiate.
I trust in the process of wealth creation and enjoy every step.
Abundance is my birthright, and I claim it with confidence.
I am open to receiving unexpected financial blessings with grace.
Every day, in every way, I am growing richer and richer.
My positive mindset attracts abundance in all its forms.
Financial success enhances every aspect of my well-being.
I am grateful for the wealth that flows into my life effortlessly.
Financial prosperity is my natural state of being.
I am open to receiving wealth in expected and unexpected ways.
Money flows to me easily, and I welcome it with open arms.
I am a magnet for financial success and positive outcomes.
I am aligned with the vibration of financial abundance.
I attract wealth effortlessly and joyfully.
I am open to the limitless possibilities of financial success.
I am a magnet for financial well-being and security.
I am grateful for the financial prosperity that fills my life.
Money comes to me in abundance, and I use it wisely.
I am open to receiving financial miracles with gratitude.
My financial abundance allows me to live a life of generosity.
Wealth flows effortlessly into my life, bringing prosperity.
I am a magnet for financial success and positive outcomes.
I am aligned with the vibration of financial abundance.
I attract wealth effortlessly and joyfully.
I am open to the limitless possibilities of financial success.
I am a magnet for financial well-being and security.
I am grateful for the financial prosperity that fills my life.
Money comes to me in abundance, and I use it wisely.
I am open to receiving financial miracles with gratitude.
I am deserving of all the prosperity life has to offer.
I am a magnet for financial opportunities, and I welcome them.

I attract financial success with every positive thought.
I am in tune with the energy of abundance and prosperity.
I am a magnet for wealth and abundance in every area of my life.
I am open to the limitless possibilities of financial success.
I am a magnet for financial well-being and security.
I am grateful for the financial prosperity that fills my life.
Money comes to me in abundance, and I use it wisely.
I am open to receiving financial miracles with gratitude.
I am deserving of all the prosperity life has to offer.
I am a magnet for financial opportunities, and I welcome them.
I attract financial success with every positive thought.
I am in tune with the energy of abundance and prosperity.
I am a magnet for wealth and abundance in every area of my life.
Financial prosperity is my natural state of being.
I am open to receiving wealth in expected and unexpected ways.
Money flows to me easily, and I welcome it with open arms.
I am open to receiving financial miracles with gratitude.
I am deserving of all the prosperity life has to offer.
I am a magnet for financial opportunities, and I welcome them.
I attract financial success with every positive thought.
I am in tune with the energy of abundance and prosperity.
I am a magnet for wealth and abundance in every area of my life.
Financial prosperity is my natural state of being.
I am open to receiving wealth in expected and unexpected ways.
Money flows to me easily, and I welcome it with open arms.
I am a magnet for financial success and positive outcomes.
I am aligned with the vibration of financial abundance.
I attract wealth effortlessly and joyfully.
I attract financial success with every positive thought.
I am in tune with the energy of abundance and prosperity.
I am a magnet for wealth and abundance in every area of my life.
Financial prosperity is my natural state of being.
I am open to receiving wealth in expected and unexpected ways.
Money flows to me easily, and I welcome it with open arms.
I am a magnet for financial success and positive outcomes.

I am aligned with the vibration of financial abundance.
I attract wealth effortlessly and joyfully.
I am open to the limitless possibilities of financial success.
I am a magnet for financial well-being and security.
I am grateful for the financial prosperity that fills my life.
Money comes to me in abundance, and I use it wisely.
I am grateful for the abundance that fills every area of my life.
I attract wealth and success with every positive thought.
Money flows to me effortlessly, and I welcome it with gratitude.
I am a magnet for financial success and positive outcomes.
I am aligned with the vibration of financial abundance.
I attract wealth effortlessly and joyfully.
I am open to the limitless possibilities of financial success.
I am a magnet for financial well-being and security.
I am grateful for the financial prosperity that fills my life.
Money comes to me in abundance, and I use it wisely.
I am open to receiving financial miracles with gratitude.
I am deserving of all the prosperity life has to offer.
I am a magnet for financial opportunities, and I welcome them.
I am open to receiving unexpected windfalls of money with gratitude.
I am deserving of all the wealth and success that comes my way.
I am financially free, and my life is filled with abundance.
I attract prosperity by maintaining a positive mindset.
Wealth is drawn to me, and I welcome it with open arms.
My positive thoughts about money create positive financial outcomes.
I am a magnet for financial miracles, and I welcome them into my life.
I am a money magnet, attracting abundance with ease.
Financial success is my birthright, and I claim it now.
My bank account is a reflection of my positive and prosperous thoughts.
I release any limiting beliefs about money and embrace my financial power.
I am open to receiving wealth beyond my wildest dreams.
Money is a tool that amplifies my positive impact on the world.
I attract financial opportunities effortlessly and naturally.
Every dollar I spend circulates and comes back to me multiplied.
My financial goals are achievable, and I pursue them with determination.

I release all fear and doubt about money, embracing abundance.

I am a wise steward of my finances, making sound and beneficial decisions.

My income is constantly increasing, and I welcome financial growth.

I am a magnet for lucrative opportunities that lead to wealth.

Financial success is a journey, and I am on the path to prosperity.

I attract wealth by consistently providing value to others.

Money comes to me effortlessly, supporting my dreams and desires.

I attract financial opportunities that align with my passions.

My wealth expands as I contribute positively to the world.

Money is a powerful force for good in my life and the lives of others.

I am open to receiving wealth from known and unknown channels.

I radiate confidence in my ability to accumulate wealth.

Financial prosperity is a natural outcome of my positive mindset.

I am a magnet for abundance, attracting it effortlessly.

I trust that the universe is conspiring to bring me financial success.

My thoughts are in alignment with the frequency of wealth.

Wealth flows to me in expected and unexpected ways.

I am a beacon of prosperity, attracting limitless abundance.

I am a magnet for financial success and positive outcomes.

I am aligned with the vibration of financial abundance.

I attract wealth effortlessly and joyfully.

I am open to the limitless possibilities of financial success.

I am a magnet for financial well-being and security.

I am grateful for the financial prosperity that fills my life.

Money comes to me in abundance, and I use it wisely.

I am open to receiving financial miracles with gratitude.

I am deserving of all the prosperity life has to offer.

I am a magnet for financial opportunities, and I welcome them.

I attract financial success with every positive thought.

I am in tune with the energy of abundance and prosperity.

I am a magnet for wealth and abundance in every area of my life.

I am deserving of all the prosperity life has to offer.

I am a magnet for financial opportunities, and I welcome them.
I attract financial success with every positive thought.
I am in tune with the energy of abundance and prosperity.
I am a magnet for wealth and abundance in every area of my life.
Financial prosperity is my natural state of being.
I am open to receiving wealth in expected and unexpected ways.
Money flows to me easily, and I welcome it with open arms.
I am a magnet for financial success and positive outcomes.
I am aligned with the vibration of financial abundance.
I attract wealth effortlessly and joyfully.
I am open to the limitless possibilities of financial success.
I am a magnet for financial well-being and security.
I am grateful for the financial prosperity that fills my life.
Money comes to me in abundance, and I use it wisely.
I am open to receiving financial miracles with gratitude.
I am deserving of all the prosperity life has to offer.
I am a magnet for financial opportunities, and I welcome them.
I attract financial success with every positive thought.
I am in tune with the energy of abundance and prosperity.
I am a magnet for wealth and abundance in every area of my life.
Financial prosperity is my natural state of being.
I am open to receiving wealth in expected and unexpected ways.
Money flows to me easily, and I welcome it with open arms.
I am in tune with the energy of abundance and prosperity.
I am a magnet for wealth and abundance in every area of my life.
Financial prosperity is my natural state of being.
I am open to receiving wealth in expected and unexpected ways.
Money flows to me easily, and I welcome it with open arms.
I am a magnet for financial success and positive outcomes.
I am aligned with the vibration of financial abundance.
I attract wealth effortlessly and joyfully.
I am open to the limitless possibilities of financial success.
I am a magnet for financial well-being and security.
I am grateful for the financial prosperity that fills my life.
Money comes to me in abundance, and I use it wisely.

I am open to receiving financial miracles with gratitude.
I attract financial opportunities that align with my purpose.
I am open to receiving wealth from diverse and creative sources.
Money flows to me easily, and I use it wisely.
I am aligned with the energy of abundance and financial well-being.
I attract positive and abundant financial experiences.
I am a magnet for attracting financial success and fulfillment.
I am grateful for the wealth and abundance in my life.
Money comes to me in abundance, and I use it to create positive change.
I am open to receiving financial miracles with gratitude.
I am deserving of all the prosperity life has to offer.
I am a magnet for financial opportunities, and I welcome them.
I attract financial success with every positive thought.
I attract wealth by staying focused on my goals and aspirations.
My mind is attuned to the frequency of financial prosperity.
I am a channel through which wealth flows effortlessly.
I attract financial success with every breath I take.
I am worthy of receiving unlimited wealth and abundance.
Money is a positive and abundant part of my life.
I welcome financial success into every area of my life.
I am open to receiving unlimited prosperity and abundance.
I am a magnet for financial prosperity, and it flows to me effortlessly.
Wealth and success are drawn to me, and I welcome them joyfully.
I am deserving of all the financial prosperity that comes my way.
My thoughts about money create a positive and abundant reality.
I welcome financial blessings with open arms and gratitude.
My financial situation is improving beyond my wildest dreams.
I trust the process of wealth creation and abundance.
I attract money with love and positive intentions.
Financial opportunities are drawn to me like a magnet.
I release any fear or doubt about my ability to accumulate wealth.
My wealth is a reflection of my positive thoughts and actions.
I attract prosperity by maintaining a mindset of abundance.
Money is a tool that empowers me to live my best life.
I am open to receiving wealth from known and unknown sources.

I am a magnet for attracting financial security and stability.
Financial success is mine to claim, and I claim it now.

My financial success serves as inspiration for others.
I trust in my ability to create unlimited wealth.
Money is a positive force, and it enriches every aspect of my life.
I am in harmony with the energy of financial well-being.
I am a magnet for attracting lucrative financial opportunities.
I am open to receiving unexpected windfalls of money.
My bank account reflects the abundance in my life.
I am grateful for the wealth that continuously manifests for me.
I am aligned with the universal flow of prosperity.
Money comes to me easily, and I am open to receiving it.

I attract financial success with every positive thought I think.

I am a magnet for wealth, and I allow it to flow freely.

Wealth constantly flows into my life with ease.

I trust that the universe is conspiring to bring me wealth.

I am open to receiving money from various channels.

My financial mindset is one of prosperity and abundance.

I attract financial opportunities effortlessly and naturally.

I am a magnet for positive financial outcomes.

Money is a source of joy and fulfillment in my life.

I welcome financial prosperity as a constant companion.

My wealth is a reflection of the value I provide to the world.

I attract wealth with grace and gratitude.

Financial success is my destiny, and I embrace it fully.

I am open to receiving wealth in ways I may not have imagined.

Abundance flows to me, and I am deserving of it.

I attract financial opportunities that align with my passions.

Money comes to me in abundance, and I use it wisely.

I am open to receiving financial miracles with gratitude.

I am deserving of all the prosperity life has to offer.

I am a magnet for financial opportunities, and I welcome them.

I attract financial success with every positive thought.

I am in tune with the energy of abundance and prosperity.

I am a magnet for wealth and abundance in every area of my life.

Financial prosperity is my natural state of being.

I am open to receiving wealth in expected and unexpected ways.

Money flows to me easily, and I welcome it

Opportunities for financial growth are abundant in my life.

I radiate confidence in my ability to attract wealth.

My financial goals are achievable and within reach.

I am a magnet for financial well-being and security.

I am grateful for the financial prosperity that fills my life.

Money comes to me in abundance, and I use it wisely.

I am open to receiving financial miracles with gratitude.

I am deserving of all the prosperity life has to offer.

I am a magnet for financial opportunities, and I welcome them.

I attract financial success with every positive thought.
I am in tune with the energy of abundance and prosperity.
I am a magnet for wealth and abundance in every area of my life.
Financial prosperity is my natural state of being.
I am open to receiving wealth in expected and unexpected ways.
Money flows to me easily, and I welcome it with open arms.
I am a magnet for financial success and positive outcomes.
I am aligned with the vibration of financial abundance.
I attract wealth effortlessly and joyfully.
I am open to the limitless possibilities of financial success.
I am deserving of all the prosperity life has to offer.
I am a magnet for financial opportunities, and I welcome them.
I attract financial success with every positive thought.
I am in tune with the energy of abundance and prosperity.
I am a magnet for wealth and abundance in every area of my life.
Financial prosperity is my natural state of being.
I am open to receiving wealth in expected and unexpected ways.
Money flows to me easily, and I welcome it with open arms.
I am a magnet for financial success and positive outcomes.
I am aligned with the vibration of financial abundance.
I attract wealth effortlessly and joyfully.
I am open to the limitless possibilities of financial success.
Wealth and success are drawn to me, and I welcome them joyfully.
I am worthy of a life filled with financial abundance.
Money is a tool that empowers me to live my best life.
I am open to receiving wealth from diverse and creative sources.
Financial success is a natural expression of my positive energy.
I attract financial opportunities effortlessly and naturally.
Money flows to me easily, and I use it wisely.
I am aligned with the energy of abundance and financial well-being.
I attract positive and abundant financial experiences.
I am a magnet for attracting financial success and fulfillment.
I am grateful for the wealth and abundance in my life.
Money comes to me in abundance, and I use it wisely.
I am open to receiving financial miracles with gratitude.

I am open to receiving wealth from known and unknown sources.
I am a magnet for financial security and stability.
Financial success is mine to claim, and I claim it now.
I attract wealth by staying focused on my goals and aspirations.
My mind is attuned to the frequency of financial prosperity.
I am a channel through which wealth flows effortlessly.
I attract financial success with every positive thought I think.
I am worthy of receiving unlimited wealth and abundance.
Money is a positive and abundant part of my life.
I welcome financial success into every area of my life.
I am open to receiving unlimited prosperity and abundance.
I am a magnet for financial prosperity, and it flows to me effortlessly.
My financial success inspires others to pursue their dreams.
I am open to receiving unexpected windfalls of money with joy.
I am a magnet for financial opportunities that align with my purpose.
Money flows to me easily, and I am open to receiving it.
I am grateful for the financial blessings that enrich my life.
I am a conduit for financial abundance, and it flows through me.

I attract wealth with grace and gratitude, creating a positive cycle.
I am aligned with the universal flow of prosperity and success.
Financial opportunities are drawn to me like a magnet.
My financial situation is improving beyond my wildest dreams.
I trust in my ability to create unlimited wealth and abundance.
I attract financial success with ease and joy.
Wealth flows into my life like a river, carrying blessings.
I am open to receiving wealth in ways beyond my imagination.
I am a magnet for lucrative opportunities that align with my goals.
My wealth grows as I invest in my personal and professional development.
I release any fear of financial limitations and embrace abundance.
I am financially free, allowing me to live life on my terms.
Money is a positive force in my life, providing limitless possibilities.
I am in harmony with the energy of wealth and abundance.

I attract prosperity with every positive thought I cultivate.
Wealth is an integral part of my life, and it manifests effortlessly.
I am open to receiving wealth from unlimited sources.
My thoughts about money create a reality of prosperity.
I am a magnet for financial success, and I welcome it graciously.
Money is a tool for positive transformation in my life and the world.
I attract financial opportunities effortlessly and gracefully.
Wealth is my natural state, and I allow it to flow abundantly.
I am a money magnet, attracting wealth from all directions.

My financial success is a reflection of my positive mindset.
Abundance is drawn to me, and I accept it with gratitude.
Money is a resource that allows me to live life to the fullest.
I am deserving of all the wealth and prosperity life offers.
My bank account is a reservoir of abundance, constantly replenishing.
My financial goals are ambitious, and I achieve them with ease.
I attract money with love and gratitude, and it multiplies.
I am aligned with the energy of prosperity and success.
Money is a positive force, and I use it to create positive change.
My income grows consistently, allowing me to fulfill my dreams.
I am a magnet for financial opportunities that elevate my life.
Wealth is my constant companion, guiding me to new heights.
I attract financial security and abundance with each breath.
I release any resistance to receiving wealth and embrace abundance.
My financial wealth allows me to contribute to the well-being of others.
I am a wise steward of my resources, making empowered choices.
I am a magnet for financial wisdom and make sound investment decisions.
I attract lucrative opportunities that align with my purpose.
Money is a source of joy and fulfillment in my life.
My bank account is a reflection of the positive energy I radiate.
I trust in the process of wealth creation and enjoy every step.
Abundance is my birthright, and I claim it with confidence.
I am open to receiving unexpected financial blessings with grace.
Every day, in every way, I am growing richer and richer.
My positive mindset attracts abundance in all its forms.
Financial success enhances every aspect of my well-being.
I am grateful for the wealth that flows into my life effortlessly.
Financial prosperity is my natural state of being.
I am open to receiving wealth in expected and unexpected ways.
Money flows to me easily, and I welcome it with open arms.
I am a magnet for financial success and positive outcomes.
I am aligned with the vibration of financial abundance.
I attract wealth effortlessly and joyfully.
I am open to the limitless possibilities of financial success.
I am a magnet for financial well-being and security.

I am grateful for the financial prosperity that fills my life.
Money comes to me in abundance, and I use it wisely.
I am open to receiving financial miracles with gratitude.
My financial abundance allows me to live a life of generosity.
Wealth flows effortlessly into my life, bringing prosperity.
I am a magnet for financial success and positive outcomes.
I am aligned with the vibration of financial abundance.
I attract wealth effortlessly and joyfully.
I am open to the limitless possibilities of financial success.
I am a magnet for financial well-being and security.
I am grateful for the financial prosperity that fills my life.
Money comes to me in abundance, and I use it wisely.
I am open to receiving financial miracles with gratitude.
I am deserving of all the prosperity life has to offer.
I am a magnet for financial opportunities, and I welcome them.
I attract financial success with every positive thought.
I am in tune with the energy of abundance and prosperity.
I am a magnet for wealth and abundance in every area of my life.
I am open to the limitless possibilities of financial success.
I am a magnet for financial well-being and security.
I am grateful for the financial prosperity that fills my life.
Money comes to me in abundance, and I use it wisely.
I am open to receiving financial miracles with gratitude.
I am deserving of all the prosperity life has to offer.
I am a magnet for financial opportunities, and I welcome them.
I attract financial success with every positive thought.
I am in tune with the energy of abundance and prosperity.
I am a magnet for wealth and abundance in every area of my life.
Financial prosperity is my natural state of being.
I am open to receiving wealth in expected and unexpected ways.
Money flows to me easily, and I welcome it with open arms.
I am open to receiving financial miracles with gratitude.
I am deserving of all the prosperity life has to offer.
I am a magnet for financial opportunities, and I welcome them.
I attract financial success with every positive thought.

I am in tune with the energy of abundance and prosperity.
I am a magnet for wealth and abundance in every area of my life.
Financial prosperity is my natural state of being.
I am open to receiving wealth in expected and unexpected ways.
Money flows to me easily, and I welcome it with open arms.
I am a magnet for financial success and positive outcomes.
I am aligned with the vibration of financial abundance.
I attract wealth effortlessly and joyfully.
I attract financial success with every positive thought.
I am in tune with the energy of abundance and prosperity.
I am a magnet for wealth and abundance in every area of my life.
Financial prosperity is my natural state of being.
I am open to receiving wealth in expected and unexpected ways.
Money flows to me easily, and I welcome it with open arms.
I am a magnet for financial success and positive outcomes.
I am aligned with the vibration of financial abundance.
I attract wealth effortlessly and joyfully.
I am open to the limitless possibilities of financial success.
I am a magnet for financial well-being and security.
I am grateful for the financial prosperity that fills my life.
Money comes to me in abundance, and I use it wisely.
I am grateful for the abundance that fills every area of my life.
I attract wealth and success with every positive thought.
Money flows to me effortlessly, and I welcome it with gratitude.
I am a magnet for financial success and positive outcomes.
I am aligned with the vibration of financial abundance.
I attract wealth effortlessly and joyfully.
I am open to the limitless possibilities of financial success.
I am a magnet for financial well-being and security.
I am grateful for the financial prosperity that fills my life.
Money comes to me in abundance, and I use it wisely.
I am open to receiving financial miracles with gratitude.
I am deserving of all the prosperity life has to offer.
I am a magnet for financial opportunities, and I welcome them.
I am open to receiving unexpected windfalls of money with gratitude.

I am deserving of all the wealth and success that comes my way.
I am financially free, and my life is filled with abundance.
I attract prosperity by maintaining a positive mindset.
Wealth is drawn to me, and I welcome it with open arms.
My positive thoughts about money create positive financial outcomes.
I am a magnet for financial miracles, and I welcome them into my life.
I am a money magnet, attracting abundance with ease.
Financial success is my birthright, and I claim it now.
My bank account is a reflection of my positive and prosperous thoughts.
I release any limiting beliefs about money and embrace my financial power.
I am open to receiving wealth beyond my wildest dreams.
Money is a tool that amplifies my positive impact on the world.
I attract financial opportunities effortlessly and naturally.
Every dollar I spend circulates and comes back to me multiplied.
My financial goals are achievable, and I pursue them with determination.
I release all fear and doubt about money, embracing abundance.
I am a wise steward of my finances, making sound and beneficial decisions.
My income is constantly increasing, and I welcome financial growth.
I am a magnet for lucrative opportunities that lead to wealth.
Financial success is a journey, and I am on the path to prosperity.
I attract wealth by consistently providing value to others.
Money comes to me effortlessly, supporting my dreams and desires.
I attract financial opportunities that align with my passions.
My wealth expands as I contribute positively to the world.
Money is a powerful force for good in my life and the lives of others.
I am open to receiving wealth from known and unknown channels.
I radiate confidence in my ability to accumulate wealth.
Financial prosperity is a natural outcome of my positive mindset.
I am a magnet for abundance, attracting it effortlessly.
I trust that the universe is conspiring to bring me financial success.
My thoughts are in alignment with the frequency of wealth.
Wealth flows to me in expected and unexpected ways.
I am a beacon of prosperity, attracting limitless abundance.
I am a magnet for financial success and positive outcomes.
I am aligned with the vibration of financial abundance.

I attract wealth effortlessly and joyfully.
I am open to the limitless possibilities of financial success.
I am a magnet for financial well-being and security.
I am grateful for the financial prosperity that fills my life.
Money comes to me in abundance, and I use it wisely.
I am open to receiving financial miracles with gratitude.
I am deserving of all the prosperity life has to offer.
I am a magnet for financial opportunities, and I welcome them.
I attract financial success with every positive thought.
I am in tune with the energy of abundance and prosperity.
I am a magnet for wealth and abundance in every area of my life.
I am deserving of all the prosperity life has to offer.

I am a magnet for financial opportunities, and I welcome them.
I attract financial success with every positive thought.
I am in tune with the energy of abundance and prosperity.
I am a magnet for wealth and abundance in every area of my life.
Financial prosperity is my natural state of being.
I am open to receiving wealth in expected and unexpected ways.
Money flows to me easily, and I welcome it with open arms.
I am a magnet for financial success and positive outcomes.
I am aligned with the vibration of financial abundance.
I attract wealth effortlessly and joyfully.
I am open to the limitless possibilities of financial success.
I am a magnet for financial well-being and security.
I am grateful for the financial prosperity that fills my life.
Money comes to me in abundance, and I use it wisely.
I am open to receiving financial miracles with gratitude.
I am deserving of all the prosperity life has to offer.
I am a magnet for financial opportunities, and I welcome them.
I attract financial success with every positive thought.
I am in tune with the energy of abundance and prosperity.
I am a magnet for wealth and abundance in every area of my life.
Financial prosperity is my natural state of being.
I am open to receiving wealth in expected and unexpected ways.
Money flows to me easily, and I welcome it with open arms.
I am in tune with the energy of abundance and prosperity.
I am a magnet for wealth and abundance in every area of my life.
Financial prosperity is my natural state of being.
I am open to receiving wealth in expected and unexpected ways.
Money flows to me easily, and I welcome it with open arms.
I am a magnet for financial success and positive outcomes.
I am aligned with the vibration of financial abundance.
I attract wealth effortlessly and joyfully.
I am open to the limitless possibilities of financial success.
I am a magnet for financial well-being and security.
I am grateful for the financial prosperity that fills my life.
Money comes to me in abundance, and I use it wisely.

I am open to receiving financial miracles with gratitude.
I attract financial opportunities that align with my purpose.
I am open to receiving wealth from diverse and creative sources.
Money flows to me easily, and I use it wisely.
I am aligned with the energy of abundance and financial well-being.
I attract positive and abundant financial experiences.
I am a magnet for attracting financial success and fulfillment.
I am grateful for the wealth and abundance in my life.
Money comes to me in abundance, and I use it to create positive change.
I am open to receiving financial miracles with gratitude.
I am deserving of all the prosperity life has to offer.
I am a magnet for financial opportunities, and I welcome them.
I attract financial success with every positive thought.
I attract wealth by staying focused on my goals and aspirations.
My mind is attuned to the frequency of financial prosperity.
I am a channel through which wealth flows effortlessly.
I attract financial success with every breath I take.
I am worthy of receiving unlimited wealth and abundance.
Money is a positive and abundant part of my life.
I welcome financial success into every area of my life.
I am open to receiving unlimited prosperity and abundance.
I am a magnet for financial prosperity, and it flows to me effortlessly.
Wealth and success are drawn to me, and I welcome them joyfully.
I am deserving of all the financial prosperity that comes my way.
My thoughts about money create a positive and abundant reality.
I welcome financial blessings with open arms and gratitude.
My financial situation is improving beyond my wildest dreams.
I trust the process of wealth creation and abundance.
I attract money with love and positive intentions.
Financial opportunities are drawn to me like a magnet.
I release any fear or doubt about my ability to accumulate wealth.
My wealth is a reflection of my positive thoughts and actions.
I attract prosperity by maintaining a mindset of abundance.
Money is a tool that empowers me to live my best life.
I am open to receiving wealth from known and unknown sources.

I am a magnet for attracting financial security and stability.
Financial success is mine to claim, and I claim it now.
My financial success serves as inspiration for others.
I trust in my ability to create unlimited wealth.
Money is a positive force, and it enriches every aspect of my life.
I am in harmony with the energy of financial well-being.
I am a magnet for attracting lucrative financial opportunities.
I am open to receiving unexpected windfalls of money.
My bank account reflects the abundance in my life.
I am grateful for the wealth that continuously manifests for me.
I am aligned with the universal flow of prosperity.
Money comes to me easily, and I am open to receiving it.
I attract financial success with every positive thought I think.
I am a magnet for wealth, and I allow it to flow freely.
Wealth constantly flows into my life with ease.
I trust that the universe is conspiring to bring me wealth.
I am open to receiving money from various channels.
My financial mindset is one of prosperity and abundance.
I attract financial opportunities effortlessly and naturally.
I am a magnet for positive financial outcomes.
Money is a source of joy and fulfillment in my life.
I welcome financial prosperity as a constant companion.
My wealth is a reflection of the value I provide to the world.
I attract wealth with grace and gratitude.
Financial success is my destiny, and I embrace it fully.
I am open to receiving wealth in ways I may not have imagined.
Abundance flows to me, and I am deserving of it.
I attract financial opportunities that align with my passions.
Money comes to me in abundance, and I use it wisely.
I am open to receiving financial miracles with gratitude.
I am deserving of all the prosperity life has to offer.
I am a magnet for financial opportunities, and I welcome them.
I attract financial success with every positive thought.
I am in tune with the energy of abundance and prosperity.
I am a magnet for wealth and abundance in every area of my life.

Financial prosperity is my natural state of being.
I am open to receiving wealth in expected and unexpected ways.
Money flows to me easily, and I welcome it
Opportunities for financial growth are abundant in my life.
I radiate confidence in my ability to attract wealth.
My financial goals are achievable and within reach.
Wealth and success are drawn to me, and I welcome them joyfully.
I am worthy of a life filled with financial abundance.
Money is a tool that empowers me to live my best life.
I am open to receiving wealth from diverse and creative sources.
Financial success is a natural expression of my positive energy.
I attract financial opportunities effortlessly and naturally.
Money flows to me easily, and I use it wisely.
I am aligned with the energy of abundance and financial well-being.
I attract positive and abundant financial experiences.
I am a magnet for attracting financial success and fulfillment.
I am grateful for the wealth and abundance in my life.
Money comes to me in abundance, and I use it wisely.
I am open to receiving financial miracles with gratitude.
I am open to receiving wealth from known and unknown sources.
I am a magnet for financial security and stability.
Financial success is mine to claim, and I claim it now.
I attract wealth by staying focused on my goals and aspirations.
My mind is attuned to the frequency of financial prosperity.
I am a channel through which wealth flows effortlessly.
I attract financial success with every positive thought I think.
I am worthy of receiving unlimited wealth and abundance.
Money is a positive and abundant part of my life.
I welcome financial success into every area of my life.
I am open to receiving unlimited prosperity and abundance.
I am a magnet for financial prosperity, and it flows to me effortlessly.
My financial success inspires others to pursue their dreams.
I am open to receiving unexpected windfalls of money with joy.
I am a magnet for financial opportunities that align with my purpose.
Money flows to me easily, and I am open to receiving it.

I am grateful for the financial blessings that enrich my life.

I am a conduit for financial abundance, and it flows through me.

I attract wealth with grace and gratitude, creating a positive cycle.

I am aligned with the universal flow of prosperity and success.

Financial opportunities are drawn to me like a magnet.

My financial situation is improving beyond my wildest dreams.

I trust in my ability to create unlimited wealth and abundance.

I attract financial success with ease and joy.

Wealth flows into my life like a river, carrying blessings.

I am open to receiving wealth in ways beyond my imagination.

I am a magnet for lucrative opportunities that align with my goals.

My wealth grows as I invest in my personal and professional development.

I release any fear of financial limitations and embrace abundance.

I am financially free, allowing me to live life on my terms.

Money is a positive force in my life, providing limitless possibilities.

I am in harmony with the energy of wealth and abundance.

I attract prosperity with every positive thought I cultivate.

Wealth is an integral part of my life, and it manifests effortlessly.

I am open to receiving wealth from unlimited sources.

My thoughts about money create a reality of prosperity.

I am a magnet for financial success, and I welcome it graciously.

Money is a tool for positive transformation in my life and the world.

I attract financial opportunities effortlessly and gracefully.

Wealth is my natural state, and I allow it to flow abundantly.

I am a money magnet, attracting wealth from all directions.

My financial success is a reflection of my positive mindset.

Abundance is drawn to me, and I accept it with gratitude.

Money is a resource that allows me to live life to the fullest.

I am deserving of all the wealth and prosperity life offers.

My bank account is a reservoir of abundance, constantly replenishing.

My financial goals are ambitious, and I achieve them with ease.

I attract money with love and gratitude, and it multiplies.

I am aligned with the energy of prosperity and success.

Money is a positive force, and I use it to create positive change.

My income grows consistently, allowing me to fulfill my dreams.

I am a magnet for financial opportunities that elevate my life.
Wealth is my constant companion, guiding me to new heights.
I attract financial security and abundance with each breath.
I release any resistance to receiving wealth and embrace abundance.
My financial wealth allows me to contribute to the well-being of others.
I am a wise steward of my resources, making empowered choices.
I am a magnet for financial wisdom and make sound investment decisions.
I attract lucrative opportunities that align with my purpose.
Money is a source of joy and fulfillment in my life.
My bank account is a reflection of the positive energy I radiate.
I trust in the process of wealth creation and enjoy every step.
Abundance is my birthright, and I claim it with confidence.
I am open to receiving unexpected financial blessings with grace.
Every day, in every way, I am growing richer and richer.
My positive mindset attracts abundance in all its forms.
Financial success enhances every aspect of my well-being.
I am grateful for the wealth that flows into my life effortlessly.
Financial prosperity is my natural state of being.
I am open to receiving wealth in expected and unexpected ways.
Money flows to me easily, and I welcome it with open arms.
I am a magnet for financial success and positive outcomes.
I am aligned with the vibration of financial abundance.
I attract wealth effortlessly and joyfully.
I am open to the limitless possibilities of financial success.
I am a magnet for financial well-being and security.
I am grateful for the financial prosperity that fills my life.
Money comes to me in abundance, and I use it wisely.
I am open to receiving financial miracles with gratitude.
My financial abundance allows me to live a life of generosity.
Wealth flows effortlessly into my life, bringing prosperity.
I am a magnet for financial success and positive outcomes.
I am aligned with the vibration of financial abundance.
I attract wealth effortlessly and joyfully.
I am open to the limitless possibilities of financial success.
I am a magnet for financial well-being and security.

I am grateful for the financial prosperity that fills my life.
Money comes to me in abundance, and I use it wisely.
I am open to receiving financial miracles with gratitude.
I am deserving of all the prosperity life has to offer.
I am a magnet for financial opportunities, and I welcome them.
I attract financial success with every positive thought.
I am in tune with the energy of abundance and prosperity.
I am a magnet for wealth and abundance in every area of my life.
I am open to the limitless possibilities of financial success.
I am a magnet for financial well-being and security.
I am grateful for the financial prosperity that fills my life.
Money comes to me in abundance, and I use it wisely.
I am open to receiving financial miracles with gratitude.

I am deserving of all the prosperity life has to offer.
I am a magnet for financial opportunities, and I welcome them.
I attract financial success with every positive thought.
I am in tune with the energy of abundance and prosperity.
I am a magnet for wealth and abundance in every area of my life.
Financial prosperity is my natural state of being.
I am open to receiving wealth in expected and unexpected ways.
Money flows to me easily, and I welcome it with open arms.
I am open to receiving financial miracles with gratitude.
I am deserving of all the prosperity life has to offer.
I am a magnet for financial opportunities, and I welcome them.
I attract financial success with every positive thought.
I am in tune with the energy of abundance and prosperity.
I am a magnet for wealth and abundance in every area of my life.
Financial prosperity is my natural state of being.
I am open to receiving wealth in expected and unexpected ways.
Money flows to me easily, and I welcome it with open arms.
I am a magnet for financial success and positive outcomes.
I am aligned with the vibration of financial abundance.
I attract wealth effortlessly and joyfully.
I attract financial success with every positive thought.
I am in tune with the energy of abundance and prosperity.
I am a magnet for wealth and abundance in every area of my life.
Financial prosperity is my natural state of being.
I am open to receiving wealth in expected and unexpected ways.
Money flows to me easily, and I welcome it with open arms.
I am a magnet for financial success and positive outcomes.
I am aligned with the vibration of financial abundance.
I attract wealth effortlessly and joyfully.
I am open to the limitless possibilities of financial success.
I am a magnet for financial well-being and security.
I am grateful for the financial prosperity that fills my life.
Money comes to me in abundance, and I use it wisely.
I am grateful for the abundance that fills every area of my life.
I attract wealth and success with every positive thought.

Money flows to me effortlessly, and I welcome it with gratitude.

I am a magnet for financial success and positive outcomes.

I am aligned with the vibration of financial abundance.

I attract wealth effortlessly and joyfully.

I am open to the limitless possibilities of financial success.

I am a magnet for financial well-being and security.

I am grateful for the financial prosperity that fills my life.

Money comes to me in abundance, and I use it wisely.

I am open to receiving financial miracles with gratitude.

I am deserving of all the prosperity life has to offer.

I am a magnet for financial opportunities, and I welcome them.

I am open to receiving unexpected windfalls of money with gratitude.

I am deserving of all the wealth and success that comes my way.

I am financially free, and my life is filled with abundance.

I attract prosperity by maintaining a positive mindset.

Wealth is drawn to me, and I welcome it with open arms.

My positive thoughts about money create positive financial outcomes.

I am a magnet for financial miracles, and I welcome them into my life.

I am a money magnet, attracting abundance with ease.

Financial success is my birthright, and I claim it now.

My bank account is a reflection of my positive and prosperous thoughts.

I release any limiting beliefs about money and embrace my financial power.

I am open to receiving wealth beyond my wildest dreams.

Money is a tool that amplifies my positive impact on the world.

I attract financial opportunities effortlessly and naturally.

Every dollar I spend circulates and comes back to me multiplied.

My financial goals are achievable, and I pursue them with determination.

I release all fear and doubt about money, embracing abundance.

I am a wise steward of my finances, making sound and beneficial decisions.

My income is constantly increasing, and I welcome financial growth.

I am a magnet for lucrative opportunities that lead to wealth.

Financial success is a journey, and I am on the path to prosperity.

I attract wealth by consistently providing value to others.

Money comes to me effortlessly, supporting my dreams and desires.

I attract financial opportunities that align with my passions.
My wealth expands as I contribute positively to the world.
Money is a powerful force for good in my life and the lives of others.
I am open to receiving wealth from known and unknown channels.
I radiate confidence in my ability to accumulate wealth.
Financial prosperity is a natural outcome of my positive mindset.
I am a magnet for abundance, attracting it effortlessly.
I trust that the universe is conspiring to bring me financial success.
My thoughts are in alignment with the frequency of wealth.
Wealth flows to me in expected and unexpected ways.
I am a beacon of prosperity, attracting limitless abundance.
I am a magnet for financial success and positive outcomes.
I am aligned with the vibration of financial abundance.
I attract wealth effortlessly and joyfully.
I am open to the limitless possibilities of financial success.
I am a magnet for financial well-being and security.
I am grateful for the financial prosperity that fills my life.
Money comes to me in abundance, and I use it wisely.
I am open to receiving financial miracles with gratitude.
I am deserving of all the prosperity life has to offer.
I am a magnet for financial opportunities, and I welcome them.
I attract financial success with every positive thought.
I am in tune with the energy of abundance and prosperity.
I am a magnet for wealth and abundance in every area of my life.
I am deserving of all the prosperity life has to offer.
I am a magnet for financial opportunities, and I welcome them.
I attract financial success with every positive thought.
I am in tune with the energy of abundance and prosperity.
I am a magnet for wealth and abundance in every area of my life.
Financial prosperity is my natural state of being.
I am open to receiving wealth in expected and unexpected ways.
Money flows to me easily, and I welcome it with open arms.
I am a magnet for financial success and positive outcomes.
I am aligned with the vibration of financial abundance.
I attract wealth effortlessly and joyfully.

I am open to the limitless possibilities of financial success.
I am a magnet for financial well-being and security.
I am grateful for the financial prosperity that fills my life.
Money comes to me in abundance, and I use it wisely.
I am open to receiving financial miracles with gratitude.
I am deserving of all the prosperity life has to offer.
I am a magnet for financial opportunities, and I welcome them.
I attract financial success with every positive thought.
I am in tune with the energy of abundance and prosperity.
I am a magnet for wealth and abundance in every area of my life.
Financial prosperity is my natural state of being.
I am open to receiving wealth in expected and unexpected ways.
Money flows to me easily, and I welcome it with open arms.
I am in tune with the energy of abundance and prosperity.
I am a magnet for wealth and abundance in every area of my life.
Financial prosperity is my natural state of being.
I am open to receiving wealth in expected and unexpected ways.
Money flows to me easily, and I welcome it with open arms.
I am a magnet for financial success and positive outcomes.
I am aligned with the vibration of financial abundance.
I attract wealth effortlessly and joyfully.
I am open to the limitless possibilities of financial success.
I am a magnet for financial well-being and security.
I am grateful for the financial prosperity that fills my life.
Money comes to me in abundance, and I use it wisely.
I am open to receiving financial miracles with gratitude.
I attract financial opportunities that align with my purpose.
I am open to receiving wealth from diverse and creative sources.
Money flows to me easily, and I use it wisely.
I am aligned with the energy of abundance and financial well-being.
I attract positive and abundant financial experiences.
I am a magnet for attracting financial success and fulfillment.
I am grateful for the wealth and abundance in my life.
Money comes to me in abundance, and I use it to create positive change.
I am open to receiving financial miracles with gratitude.

I am deserving of all the prosperity life has to offer.
I am a magnet for financial opportunities, and I welcome them.
I attract financial success with every positive thought.
I attract wealth by staying focused on my goals and aspirations.
My mind is attuned to the frequency of financial prosperity.
I am a channel through which wealth flows effortlessly.
I attract financial success with every breath I take.
I am worthy of receiving unlimited wealth and abundance.
Money is a positive and abundant part of my life.
I welcome financial success into every area of my life.
I am open to receiving unlimited prosperity and abundance.
I am a magnet for financial prosperity, and it flows to me effortlessly.
Wealth and success are drawn to me, and I welcome them joyfully.
I am deserving of all the financial prosperity that comes my way.
My thoughts about money create a positive and abundant reality.
I welcome financial blessings with open arms and gratitude.
My financial situation is improving beyond my wildest dreams.
I trust the process of wealth creation and abundance.
I attract money with love and positive intentions.
Financial opportunities are drawn to me like a magnet.
I release any fear or doubt about my ability to accumulate wealth.
My wealth is a reflection of my positive thoughts and actions.
I attract prosperity by maintaining a mindset of abundance.
Money is a tool that empowers me to live my best life.
I am open to receiving wealth from known and unknown sources.
I am a magnet for attracting financial security and stability.
Financial success is mine to claim, and I claim it now.
My financial success serves as inspiration for others.
I trust in my ability to create unlimited wealth.
Money is a positive force, and it enriches every aspect of my life.
I am in harmony with the energy of financial well-being.
I am a magnet for attracting lucrative financial opportunities.
I am open to receiving unexpected windfalls of money.
My bank account reflects the abundance in my life.
I am grateful for the wealth that continuously manifests for me.

I am aligned with the universal flow of prosperity.
Money comes to me easily, and I am open to receiving it.
I attract financial success with every positive thought I think.
I am a magnet for wealth, and I allow it to flow freely.
Wealth constantly flows into my life with ease.
I trust that the universe is conspiring to bring me wealth.
I am open to receiving money from various channels.
My financial mindset is one of prosperity and abundance.
I attract financial opportunities effortlessly and naturally.
I am a magnet for positive financial outcomes.
Money is a source of joy and fulfillment in my life.
I welcome financial prosperity as a constant companion.
My wealth is a reflection of the value I provide to the world.
I attract wealth with grace and gratitude.
Financial success is my destiny, and I embrace it fully.
I am open to receiving wealth in ways I may not have imagined.
Abundance flows to me, and I am deserving of it.
I attract financial opportunities that align with my passions.
Money comes to me in abundance, and I use it wisely.
I am open to receiving financial miracles with gratitude.
I am deserving of all the prosperity life has to offer.
I am a magnet for financial opportunities, and I welcome them.
I attract financial success with every positive thought.
I am in tune with the energy of abundance and prosperity.
I am a magnet for wealth and abundance in every area of my life.
Financial prosperity is my natural state of being.
I am open to receiving wealth in expected and unexpected ways.
Money flows to me easily, and I welcome it
Opportunities for financial growth are abundant in my life.
I radiate confidence in my ability to attract wealth.
My financial goals are achievable and within reach.
Wealth and success are drawn to me, and I welcome them joyfully.
I am worthy of a life filled with financial abundance.
Money is a tool that empowers me to live my best life.
I am open to receiving wealth from diverse and creative sources.

Financial success is a natural expression of my positive energy.

I attract financial opportunities effortlessly and naturally.

Money flows to me easily, and I use it wisely.

I am aligned with the energy of abundance and financial well-being.

I attract positive and abundant financial experiences.

I am a magnet for attracting financial success and fulfillment.

I am grateful for the wealth and abundance in my life.

Money comes to me in abundance, and I use it wisely.

I am open to receiving financial miracles with gratitude.

I am open to receiving wealth from known and unknown sources.

I am a magnet for financial security and stability.

Financial success is mine to claim, and I claim it now.

I attract wealth by staying focused on my goals and aspirations.

My mind is attuned to the frequency of financial prosperity.

I am a channel through which wealth flows effortlessly.

I attract financial success with every positive thought I think.

I am worthy of receiving unlimited wealth and abundance.

Money is a positive and abundant part of my life.

I welcome financial success into every area of my life.

I am open to receiving unlimited prosperity and abundance.

I am a magnet for financial prosperity, and it flows to me effortlessly.

My financial success inspires others to pursue their dreams.

I am open to receiving unexpected windfalls of money with joy.

I am a magnet for financial opportunities that align with my purpose.

Money flows to me easily, and I am open to receiving it.

I am grateful for the financial blessings that enrich my life.

I am a conduit for financial abundance, and it flows through me.

I attract wealth with grace and gratitude, creating a positive cycle.

I am aligned with the universal flow of prosperity and success.

Financial opportunities are drawn to me like a magnet.

My financial situation is improving beyond my wildest dreams.

I trust in my ability to create unlimited wealth and abundance.

I attract financial success with ease and joy.

Wealth flows into my life like a river, carrying blessings.

I am open to receiving wealth in ways beyond my imagination.

I am a magnet for lucrative opportunities that align with my goals.

My wealth grows as I invest in my personal and professional development.

I release any fear of financial limitations and embrace abundance.

I am financially free, allowing me to live life on my terms.

Money is a positive force in my life, providing limitless possibilities.

I am in harmony with the energy of wealth and abundance.

I attract prosperity with every positive thought I cultivate.

Wealth is an integral part of my life, and it manifests effortlessly.

I am open to receiving wealth from unlimited sources.

My thoughts about money create a reality of prosperity.

I am a magnet for financial success, and I welcome it graciously.

Money is a tool for positive transformation in my life and the world.

I attract financial opportunities effortlessly and gracefully.

Wealth is my natural state, and I allow it to flow abundantly.

I am a money magnet, attracting wealth from all directions.

My financial success is a reflection of my positive mindset.

Abundance is drawn to me, and I accept it with gratitude.

Money is a resource that allows me to live life to the fullest.

I am deserving of all the wealth and prosperity life offers.

My bank account is a reservoir of abundance, constantly replenishing.

My financial goals are ambitious, and I achieve them with ease.

I attract money with love and gratitude, and it multiplies.

I am aligned with the energy of prosperity and success.

Money is a positive force, and I use it to create positive change.

My income grows consistently, allowing me to fulfill my dreams.

I am a magnet for financial opportunities that elevate my life.

Wealth is my constant companion, guiding me to new heights.

I attract financial security and abundance with each breath.

I release any resistance to receiving wealth and embrace abundance.

My financial wealth allows me to contribute to the well-being of others.

I am a wise steward of my resources, making empowered choices.

I am a magnet for financial wisdom and make sound investment decisions.

I attract lucrative opportunities that align with my purpose.
Money is a source of joy and fulfillment in my life.
My bank account is a reflection of the positive energy I radiate.
I trust in the process of wealth creation and enjoy every step.
Abundance is my birthright, and I claim it with confidence.
I am open to receiving unexpected financial blessings with grace.
Every day, in every way, I am growing richer and richer.
My positive mindset attracts abundance in all its forms.
Financial success enhances every aspect of my well-being.
I am grateful for the wealth that flows into my life effortlessly.
Financial prosperity is my natural state of being.
I am open to receiving wealth in expected and unexpected ways.
Money flows to me easily, and I welcome it with open arms.
I am a magnet for financial success and positive outcomes.
I am aligned with the vibration of financial abundance.
I attract wealth effortlessly and joyfully.
I am open to the limitless possibilities of financial success.
I am a magnet for financial well-being and security.
I am grateful for the financial prosperity that fills my life.
Money comes to me in abundance, and I use it wisely.
I am open to receiving financial miracles with gratitude.
My financial abundance allows me to live a life of generosity.
Wealth flows effortlessly into my life, bringing prosperity.
I am a magnet for financial success and positive outcomes.
I am aligned with the vibration of financial abundance.
I attract wealth effortlessly and joyfully.
I am open to the limitless possibilities of financial success.
I am a magnet for financial well-being and security.
I am grateful for the financial prosperity that fills my life.
Money comes to me in abundance, and I use it wisely.
I am open to receiving financial miracles with gratitude.
I am deserving of all the prosperity life has to offer.
I am a magnet for financial opportunities, and I welcome them.
I attract financial success with every positive thought.
I am in tune with the energy of abundance and prosperity.

I am a magnet for wealth and abundance in every area of my life.
I am open to the limitless possibilities of financial success.
I am a magnet for financial well-being and security.
I am grateful for the financial prosperity that fills my life.
Money comes to me in abundance, and I use it wisely.
I am open to receiving financial miracles with gratitude.
I am deserving of all the prosperity life has to offer.
I am a magnet for financial opportunities, and I welcome them.
I attract financial success with every positive thought.
I am in tune with the energy of abundance and prosperity.
I am a magnet for wealth and abundance in every area of my life.
Financial prosperity is my natural state of being.
I am open to receiving wealth in expected and unexpected ways.
Money flows to me easily, and I welcome it with open arms.
I am open to receiving financial miracles with gratitude.
I am deserving of all the prosperity life has to offer.
I am a magnet for financial opportunities, and I welcome them.
I attract financial success with every positive thought.
I am in tune with the energy of abundance and prosperity.
I am a magnet for wealth and abundance in every area of my life.
Financial prosperity is my natural state of being.
I am open to receiving wealth in expected and unexpected ways.
Money flows to me easily, and I welcome it with open arms.
I am a magnet for financial success and positive outcomes.
I am aligned with the vibration of financial abundance.
I attract wealth effortlessly and joyfully.
I attract financial success with every positive thought.
I am in tune with the energy of abundance and prosperity.
I am a magnet for wealth and abundance in every area of my life.
Financial prosperity is my natural state of being.
I am open to receiving wealth in expected and unexpected ways.
Money flows to me easily, and I welcome it with open arms.
I am a magnet for financial success and positive outcomes.
I am aligned with the vibration of financial abundance.
I attract wealth effortlessly and joyfully.

I am open to the limitless possibilities of financial success.

I am a magnet for financial well-being and security.

I am grateful for the financial prosperity that fills my life.

Money comes to me in abundance, and I use it wisely.

I am grateful for the abundance that fills every area of my life.

I attract wealth and success with every positive thought.

Money flows to me effortlessly, and I welcome it with gratitude.

I am a magnet for financial success and positive outcomes.

I am aligned with the vibration of financial abundance.

I attract wealth effortlessly and joyfully.

I am open to the limitless possibilities of financial success.

I am a magnet for financial well-being and security.

I am grateful for the financial prosperity that fills my life.

Money comes to me in abundance, and I use it wisely.

I am open to receiving financial miracles with gratitude.

I am deserving of all the prosperity life has to offer.

I am a magnet for financial opportunities, and I welcome them.

I am open to receiving unexpected windfalls of money with gratitude.

I am deserving of all the wealth and success that comes my way.

I am financially free, and my life is filled with abundance.

I attract prosperity by maintaining a positive mindset.

Wealth is drawn to me, and I welcome it with open arms.

My positive thoughts about money create positive financial outcomes.

I am a magnet for financial miracles, and I welcome them into my life.

I am a money magnet, attracting abundance with ease.

Financial success is my birthright, and I claim it now.

My bank account is a reflection of my positive and prosperous thoughts.

I release any limiting beliefs about money and embrace my financial power.

I am open to receiving wealth beyond my wildest dreams.

Money is a tool that amplifies my positive impact on the world.

I attract financial opportunities effortlessly and naturally.

Every dollar I spend circulates and comes back to me multiplied.

My financial goals are achievable, and I pursue them with determination.

I release all fear and doubt about money, embracing abundance.

I am a wise steward of my finances, making sound and beneficial decisions.

My income is constantly increasing, and I welcome financial growth.
I am a magnet for lucrative opportunities that lead to wealth.
Financial success is a journey, and I am on the path to prosperity.
I attract wealth by consistently providing value to others.
Money comes to me effortlessly, supporting my dreams and desires.
I attract financial opportunities that align with my passions.
My wealth expands as I contribute positively to the world.
Money is a powerful force for good in my life and the lives of others.
I am open to receiving wealth from known and unknown channels.
I radiate confidence in my ability to accumulate wealth.
Financial prosperity is a natural outcome of my positive mindset.
I am a magnet for abundance, attracting it effortlessly.
I trust that the universe is conspiring to bring me financial success.
My thoughts are in alignment with the frequency of wealth.
Wealth flows to me in expected and unexpected ways.
I am a beacon of prosperity, attracting limitless abundance.
I am a magnet for financial success and positive outcomes.
I am aligned with the vibration of financial abundance.
I attract wealth effortlessly and joyfully.
I am open to the limitless possibilities of financial success.
I am a magnet for financial well-being and security.
I am grateful for the financial prosperity that fills my life.
Money comes to me in abundance, and I use it wisely.
I am open to receiving financial miracles with gratitude.
I am deserving of all the prosperity life has to offer.
I am a magnet for financial opportunities, and I welcome them.
I attract financial success with every positive thought.
I am in tune with the energy of abundance and prosperity.
I am a magnet for wealth and abundance in every area of my life.
I am deserving of all the prosperity life has to offer.
I am a magnet for financial opportunities, and I welcome them.
I attract financial success with every positive thought.
I am in tune with the energy of abundance and prosperity.
I am a magnet for wealth and abundance in every area of my life.
Financial prosperity is my natural state of being.

I am open to receiving wealth in expected and unexpected ways.
Money flows to me easily, and I welcome it with open arms.
I am a magnet for financial success and positive outcomes.
I am aligned with the vibration of financial abundance.
I attract wealth effortlessly and joyfully.
I am open to the limitless possibilities of financial success.
I am a magnet for financial well-being and security.
I am grateful for the financial prosperity that fills my life.
Money comes to me in abundance, and I use it wisely.
I am open to receiving financial miracles with gratitude.
I am deserving of all the prosperity life has to offer.
I am a magnet for financial opportunities, and I welcome them.
I attract financial success with every positive thought.
I am in tune with the energy of abundance and prosperity.
I am a magnet for wealth and abundance in every area of my life.
Financial prosperity is my natural state of being.
I am open to receiving wealth in expected and unexpected ways.
Money flows to me easily, and I welcome it with open arms.
I am in tune with the energy of abundance and prosperity.
I am a magnet for wealth and abundance in every area of my life.
Financial prosperity is my natural state of being.
I am open to receiving wealth in expected and unexpected ways.
Money flows to me easily, and I welcome it with open arms.
I am a magnet for financial success and positive outcomes.
I am aligned with the vibration of financial abundance.
I attract wealth effortlessly and joyfully.
I am open to the limitless possibilities of financial success.
I am a magnet for financial well-being and security.
I am grateful for the financial prosperity that fills my life.
Money comes to me in abundance, and I use it wisely.
I am open to receiving financial miracles with gratitude.
I attract financial opportunities that align with my purpose.
I am open to receiving wealth from diverse and creative sources.
Money flows to me easily, and I use it wisely.
I am aligned with the energy of abundance and financial well-being.

I attract positive and abundant financial experiences.

I am a magnet for attracting financial success and fulfillment.

I am grateful for the wealth and abundance in my life.

Money comes to me in abundance, and I use it to create positive change.

I am open to receiving financial miracles with gratitude.

I am deserving of all the prosperity life has to offer.

I am a magnet for financial opportunities, and I welcome them.

I attract financial success with every positive thought.

I attract wealth by staying focused on my goals and aspirations.

My mind is attuned to the frequency of financial prosperity.

I am a channel through which wealth flows effortlessly.

I attract financial success with every breath I take.

I am worthy of receiving unlimited wealth and abundance.

Money is a positive and abundant part of my life.

I welcome financial success into every area of my life.

I am open to receiving unlimited prosperity and abundance.

I am a magnet for financial prosperity, and it flows to me effortlessly.

Wealth and success are drawn to me, and I welcome them joyfully.

I am deserving of all the financial prosperity that comes my way.

My thoughts about money create a positive and abundant reality.

I welcome financial blessings with open arms and gratitude.

My financial situation is improving beyond my wildest dreams.

I trust the process of wealth creation and abundance.

I attract money with love and positive intentions.

Financial opportunities are drawn to me like a magnet.

I release any fear or doubt about my ability to accumulate wealth.

My wealth is a reflection of my positive thoughts and actions.

I attract prosperity by maintaining a mindset of abundance.

Money is a tool that empowers me to live my best life.

I am open to receiving wealth from known and unknown sources.

I am a magnet for attracting financial security and stability.

Financial success is mine to claim, and I claim it now.

My financial success serves as inspiration for others.

I trust in my ability to create unlimited wealth.

Money is a positive force, and it enriches every aspect of my life.

I am in harmony with the energy of financial well-being.
I am a magnet for attracting lucrative financial opportunities.
I am open to receiving unexpected windfalls of money.
My bank account reflects the abundance in my life.
I am grateful for the wealth that continuously manifests for me.
I am aligned with the universal flow of prosperity.
Money comes to me easily, and I am open to receiving it.
I attract financial success with every positive thought I think.
I am a magnet for wealth, and I allow it to flow freely.
Wealth constantly flows into my life with ease.
I trust that the universe is conspiring to bring me wealth.
I am open to receiving money from various channels.
My financial mindset is one of prosperity and abundance.
I attract financial opportunities effortlessly and naturally.
I am a magnet for positive financial outcomes.
Money is a source of joy and fulfillment in my life.
I welcome financial prosperity as a constant companion.
My wealth is a reflection of the value I provide to the world.
I attract wealth with grace and gratitude.
Financial success is my destiny, and I embrace it fully.
I am open to receiving wealth in ways I may not have imagined.
Abundance flows to me, and I am deserving of it.
I attract financial opportunities that align with my passions.
Money comes to me in abundance, and I use it wisely.
I am open to receiving financial miracles with gratitude.
I am deserving of all the prosperity life has to offer.
I am a magnet for financial opportunities, and I welcome them.
I attract financial success with every positive thought.
I am in tune with the energy of abundance and prosperity.
I am a magnet for wealth and abundance in every area of my life.
Financial prosperity is my natural state of being.
I am open to receiving wealth in expected and unexpected ways.
Money flows to me easily, and I welcome it
Opportunities for financial growth are abundant in my life.
I radiate confidence in my ability to attract wealth.

My financial goals are achievable and within reach.
Wealth and success are drawn to me, and I welcome them joyfully.
I am worthy of a life filled with financial abundance.
Money is a tool that empowers me to live my best life.
I am open to receiving wealth from diverse and creative sources.
Financial success is a natural expression of my positive energy.
I attract financial opportunities effortlessly and naturally.
Money flows to me easily, and I use it wisely.
I am aligned with the energy of abundance and financial well-being.
I attract positive and abundant financial experiences.
I am a magnet for attracting financial success and fulfillment.
I am grateful for the wealth and abundance in my life.
Money comes to me in abundance, and I use it wisely.
I am open to receiving financial miracles with gratitude.
I am open to receiving wealth from known and unknown sources.
I am a magnet for financial security and stability.
Financial success is mine to claim, and I claim it now.
I attract wealth by staying focused on my goals and aspirations.
My mind is attuned to the frequency of financial prosperity.
I am a channel through which wealth flows effortlessly.
I attract financial success with every positive thought I think.
I am worthy of receiving unlimited wealth and abundance.
Money is a positive and abundant part of my life.
I welcome financial success into every area of my life.
I am open to receiving unlimited prosperity and abundance.
I am a magnet for financial prosperity, and it flows to me effortlessly.
My financial success inspires others to pursue their dreams.
I am open to receiving unexpected windfalls of money with joy.
I am a magnet for financial opportunities that align with my purpose.
Money flows to me easily, and I am open to receiving it.
I am grateful for the financial blessings that enrich my life.
I am a conduit for financial abundance, and it flows through me.
I attract wealth with grace and gratitude, creating a positive cycle.
I am aligned with the universal flow of prosperity and success.
Financial opportunities are drawn to me like a magnet.

My financial situation is improving beyond my wildest dreams.
I trust in my ability to create unlimited wealth and abundance.
I attract financial success with ease and joy.
Wealth flows into my life like a river, carrying blessings.
I am open to receiving wealth in ways beyond my imagination.
I am a magnet for lucrative opportunities that align with my goals.
My wealth grows as I invest in my personal and professional development.
I release any fear of financial limitations and embrace abundance.
I am financially free, allowing me to live life on my terms.
Money is a positive force in my life, providing limitless possibilities.
I am in harmony with the energy of wealth and abundance.
I attract prosperity with every positive thought I cultivate.
Wealth is an integral part of my life, and it manifests effortlessly.
I am open to receiving wealth from unlimited sources.
My thoughts about money create a reality of prosperity.
I am a magnet for financial success, and I welcome it graciously.
Money is a tool for positive transformation in my life and the world.
I attract financial opportunities effortlessly and gracefully.
Wealth is my natural state, and I allow it to flow abundantly.
I am a money magnet, attracting wealth from all directions.
My financial success is a reflection of my positive mindset.
Abundance is drawn to me, and I accept it with gratitude.
Money is a resource that allows me to live life to the fullest.
I am deserving of all the wealth and prosperity life offers.
My bank account is a reservoir of abundance, constantly replenishing.
My financial goals are ambitious, and I achieve them with ease.
I attract money with love and gratitude, and it multiplies.
I am aligned with the energy of prosperity and success.
Money is a positive force, and I use it to create positive change.
My income grows consistently, allowing me to fulfill my dreams.
I am a magnet for financial opportunities that elevate my life.
Wealth is my constant companion, guiding me to new heights.
I attract financial security and abundance with each breath.
I release any resistance to receiving wealth and embrace abundance.
My financial wealth allows me to contribute to the well-being of others.

I am a wise steward of my resources, making empowered choices.
I am a magnet for financial wisdom and make sound investment decisions.
I attract lucrative opportunities that align with my purpose.
Money is a source of joy and fulfillment in my life.
My bank account is a reflection of the positive energy I radiate.
I trust in the process of wealth creation and enjoy every step.
Abundance is my birthright, and I claim it with confidence.
I am open to receiving unexpected financial blessings with grace.
Every day, in every way, I am growing richer and richer.
My positive mindset attracts abundance in all its forms.
Financial success enhances every aspect of my well-being.
I am grateful for the wealth that flows into my life effortlessly.
Financial prosperity is my natural state of being.
I am open to receiving wealth in expected and unexpected ways.
Money flows to me easily, and I welcome it with open arms.
I am a magnet for financial success and positive outcomes.
I am aligned with the vibration of financial abundance.
I attract wealth effortlessly and joyfully.
I am open to the limitless possibilities of financial success.
I am a magnet for financial well-being and security.
I am grateful for the financial prosperity that fills my life.
Money comes to me in abundance, and I use it wisely.
I am open to receiving financial miracles with gratitude.
My financial abundance allows me to live a life of generosity.
Wealth flows effortlessly into my life, bringing prosperity.
I am a magnet for financial success and positive outcomes.
I am aligned with the vibration of financial abundance.
I attract wealth effortlessly and joyfully.
I am open to the limitless possibilities of financial success.
I am a magnet for financial well-being and security.
I am grateful for the financial prosperity that fills my life.
Money comes to me in abundance, and I use it wisely.
I am open to receiving financial miracles with gratitude.
I am deserving of all the prosperity life has to offer.
I am a magnet for financial opportunities, and I welcome them.

I attract financial success with every positive thought.
I am in tune with the energy of abundance and prosperity.
I am a magnet for wealth and abundance in every area of my life.
I am open to the limitless possibilities of financial success.
I am a magnet for financial well-being and security.
I am grateful for the financial prosperity that fills my life.
Money comes to me in abundance, and I use it wisely.
I am open to receiving financial miracles with gratitude.
I am deserving of all the prosperity life has to offer.
I am a magnet for financial opportunities, and I welcome them.
I attract financial success with every positive thought.
I am in tune with the energy of abundance and prosperity.
I am a magnet for wealth and abundance in every area of my life.
Financial prosperity is my natural state of being.
I am open to receiving wealth in expected and unexpected ways.
Money flows to me easily, and I welcome it with open arms.
I am open to receiving financial miracles with gratitude.
I am deserving of all the prosperity life has to offer.
I am a magnet for financial opportunities, and I welcome them.
I attract financial success with every positive thought.
I am in tune with the energy of abundance and prosperity.
I am a magnet for wealth and abundance in every area of my life.
Financial prosperity is my natural state of being.
I am open to receiving wealth in expected and unexpected ways.
Money flows to me easily, and I welcome it with open arms.
I am a magnet for financial success and positive outcomes.
I am aligned with the vibration of financial abundance.
I attract wealth effortlessly and joyfully.
I attract financial success with every positive thought.
I am in tune with the energy of abundance and prosperity.
I am a magnet for wealth and abundance in every area of my life.
Financial prosperity is my natural state of being.
I am open to receiving wealth in expected and unexpected ways.
Money flows to me easily, and I welcome it with open arms.
I am a magnet for financial success and positive outcomes.

I am aligned with the vibration of financial abundance.
I attract wealth effortlessly and joyfully.
I am open to the limitless possibilities of financial success.
I am a magnet for financial well-being and security.
I am grateful for the financial prosperity that fills my life.
Money comes to me in abundance, and I use it wisely.
I am grateful for the abundance that fills every area of my life.
I attract wealth and success with every positive thought.
Money flows to me effortlessly, and I welcome it with gratitude.
I am a magnet for financial success and positive outcomes.
I am aligned with the vibration of financial abundance.
I attract wealth effortlessly and joyfully.
I am open to the limitless possibilities of financial success.
I am a magnet for financial well-being and security.
I am grateful for the financial prosperity that fills my life.
Money comes to me in abundance, and I use it wisely.
I am open to receiving financial miracles with gratitude.
I am deserving of all the prosperity life has to offer.
I am a magnet for financial opportunities, and I welcome them.
I am open to receiving unexpected windfalls of money with gratitude.
I am deserving of all the wealth and success that comes my way.
I am financially free, and my life is filled with abundance.
I attract prosperity by maintaining a positive mindset.
Wealth is drawn to me, and I welcome it with open arms.
My positive thoughts about money create positive financial outcomes.
I am a magnet for financial miracles, and I welcome them into my life.
I am a money magnet, attracting abundance with ease.
Financial success is my birthright, and I claim it now.
My bank account is a reflection of my positive and prosperous thoughts.
I release any limiting beliefs about money and embrace my financial power.
I am open to receiving wealth beyond my wildest dreams.
Money is a tool that amplifies my positive impact on the world.
I attract financial opportunities effortlessly and naturally.
Every dollar I spend circulates and comes back to me multiplied.
My financial goals are achievable, and I pursue them with determination.

I release all fear and doubt about money, embracing abundance.
I am a wise steward of my finances, making sound and beneficial decisions.
My income is constantly increasing, and I welcome financial growth.
I am a magnet for lucrative opportunities that lead to wealth.
Financial success is a journey, and I am on the path to prosperity.
I attract wealth by consistently providing value to others.
Money comes to me effortlessly, supporting my dreams and desires.
I attract financial opportunities that align with my passions.
My wealth expands as I contribute positively to the world.
Money is a powerful force for good in my life and the lives of others.
I am open to receiving wealth from known and unknown channels.
I radiate confidence in my ability to accumulate wealth.
Financial prosperity is a natural outcome of my positive mindset.
I am a magnet for abundance, attracting it effortlessly.
I trust that the universe is conspiring to bring me financial success.
My thoughts are in alignment with the frequency of wealth.
Wealth flows to me in expected and unexpected ways.
I am a beacon of prosperity, attracting limitless abundance.
I am a magnet for financial success and positive outcomes.
I am aligned with the vibration of financial abundance.
I attract wealth effortlessly and joyfully.
I am open to the limitless possibilities of financial success.
I am a magnet for financial well-being and security.
I am grateful for the financial prosperity that fills my life.
Money comes to me in abundance, and I use it wisely.
I am open to receiving financial miracles with gratitude.
I am deserving of all the prosperity life has to offer.
I am a magnet for financial opportunities, and I welcome them.
I attract financial success with every positive thought.
I am in tune with the energy of abundance and prosperity.
I am a magnet for wealth and abundance in every area of my life.
I am deserving of all the prosperity life has to offer.

I am a magnet for financial opportunities, and I welcome them.
I attract financial success with every positive thought.
I am in tune with the energy of abundance and prosperity.
I am a magnet for wealth and abundance in every area of my life.
Financial prosperity is my natural state of being.
I am open to receiving wealth in expected and unexpected ways.
Money flows to me easily, and I welcome it with open arms.
I am a magnet for financial success and positive outcomes.
I am aligned with the vibration of financial abundance.
I attract wealth effortlessly and joyfully.
I am open to the limitless possibilities of financial success.
I am a magnet for financial well-being and security.
I am grateful for the financial prosperity that fills my life.
Money comes to me in abundance, and I use it wisely.
I am open to receiving financial miracles with gratitude.
I am deserving of all the prosperity life has to offer.
I am a magnet for financial opportunities, and I welcome them.
I attract financial success with every positive thought.
I am in tune with the energy of abundance and prosperity.
I am a magnet for wealth and abundance in every area of my life.
Financial prosperity is my natural state of being.
I am open to receiving wealth in expected and unexpected ways.
Money flows to me easily, and I welcome it with open arms.
I am in tune with the energy of abundance and prosperity.
I am a magnet for wealth and abundance in every area of my life.
Financial prosperity is my natural state of being.
I am open to receiving wealth in expected and unexpected ways.
Money flows to me easily, and I welcome it with open arms.
I am a magnet for financial success and positive outcomes.
I am aligned with the vibration of financial abundance.
I attract wealth effortlessly and joyfully.
I am open to the limitless possibilities of financial success.
I am a magnet for financial well-being and security.
I am grateful for the financial prosperity that fills my life.
Money comes to me in abundance, and I use it wisely.

I am open to receiving financial miracles with gratitude.

I attract financial opportunities that align with my purpose.

I am open to receiving wealth from diverse and creative sources.

Money flows to me easily, and I use it wisely.

I am aligned with the energy of abundance and financial well-being.

I attract positive and abundant financial experiences.

I am a magnet for attracting financial success and fulfillment.

I am grateful for the wealth and abundance in my life.

Money comes to me in abundance, and I use it to create positive change.

I am open to receiving financial miracles with gratitude.

I am deserving of all the prosperity life has to offer.

I am a magnet for financial opportunities, and I welcome them.

I attract financial success with every positive thought.

I attract wealth by staying focused on my goals and aspirations.

My mind is attuned to the frequency of financial prosperity.

I am a channel through which wealth flows effortlessly.

I attract financial success with every breath I take.

I am worthy of receiving unlimited wealth and abundance.

Money is a positive and abundant part of my life.

I welcome financial success into every area of my life.

I am open to receiving unlimited prosperity and abundance.

I am a magnet for financial prosperity, and it flows to me effortlessly.

Wealth and success are drawn to me, and I welcome them joyfully.

I am deserving of all the financial prosperity that comes my way.

My thoughts about money create a positive and abundant reality.

I welcome financial blessings with open arms and gratitude.

My financial situation is improving beyond my wildest dreams.

I trust the process of wealth creation and abundance.

I attract money with love and positive intentions.

Financial opportunities are drawn to me like a magnet.

I release any fear or doubt about my ability to accumulate wealth.

My wealth is a reflection of my positive thoughts and actions.

I attract prosperity by maintaining a mindset of abundance.

Money is a tool that empowers me to live my best life.

I am open to receiving wealth from known and unknown sources.

I am a magnet for attracting financial security and stability.
Financial success is mine to claim, and I claim it now.

My financial success serves as inspiration for others.
I trust in my ability to create unlimited wealth.
Money is a positive force, and it enriches every aspect of my life.
I am in harmony with the energy of financial well-being.
I am a magnet for attracting lucrative financial opportunities.
I am open to receiving unexpected windfalls of money.
My bank account reflects the abundance in my life.
I am grateful for the wealth that continuously manifests for me.
I am aligned with the universal flow of prosperity.
Money comes to me easily, and I am open to receiving it.

I attract financial success with every positive thought I think.
I am a magnet for wealth, and I allow it to flow freely.
Wealth constantly flows into my life with ease.
I trust that the universe is conspiring to bring me wealth.
I am open to receiving money from various channels.
My financial mindset is one of prosperity and abundance.
I attract financial opportunities effortlessly and naturally.
I am a magnet for positive financial outcomes.
Money is a source of joy and fulfillment in my life.
I welcome financial prosperity as a constant companion.
My wealth is a reflection of the value I provide to the world.
I attract wealth with grace and gratitude.
Financial success is my destiny, and I embrace it fully.
I am open to receiving wealth in ways I may not have imagined.
Abundance flows to me, and I am deserving of it.
I attract financial opportunities that align with my passions.
Money comes to me in abundance, and I use it wisely.
I am open to receiving financial miracles with gratitude.
I am deserving of all the prosperity life has to offer.
I am a magnet for financial opportunities, and I welcome them.
I attract financial success with every positive thought.
I am in tune with the energy of abundance and prosperity.
I am a magnet for wealth and abundance in every area of my life.
Financial prosperity is my natural state of being.
I am open to receiving wealth in expected and unexpected ways.
Money flows to me easily, and I welcome it
Opportunities for financial growth are abundant in my life.
I radiate confidence in my ability to attract wealth.
My financial goals are achievable and within reach.